LANDED ON BLACK

ZACH FORTIER

steeleshark
press

Cover design, interior book design,
eBook design, and editing
by Blue Harvest Creative
www.blueharvestcreative.com

LANDED ON BLACK

Published by
SteeleShark Press

ISBN-13: 978-0692245330
ISBN-10: 0692245332

Visit the author at:
Website: *www.zachfortier.com*
Blog: *www.authorzachfortier.blogspot.com*
Facebook: *www.facebook.com/authorzach.fortier*
Twitter: *www.twitter.com/zachfortier1*
Goodreads: *www.goodreads.com/author/show/5164780.Zach_Fortier*

Purchase other books by Zach Fortier in print, eBook, or audio by scanning the QR code.

ZACH FORTIER

ONE DAY AFTER DUMPING A drunk on his ass for interfering in a call, an officer who used to ride with me said he never knew what I would do. I was erratic and unpredictable. Sometimes people would spit on me, and I would do nothing. At other times if someone looked at me the wrong way they would "land on black," and all hell would break loose.

Later, I realized this was because of the post-traumatic stress disorder (PTSD) I was suffering from. I was already damaged from all the shit I had experienced. The constant need to watch my back with everyone I met in every circumstance had taken its toll. The point of this book is to talk about that. How I could never believe or trust anyone or anything—sometimes not even myself.

People have repeatedly accused me of being jaded and paranoid my entire police career. Now they read the books I have written and say I am clearly jaded and see conspiracy where it doesn't exist. You decide: Am I paranoid? The streets don't lie. If your eyes are opened to the reality of what is going on around you, you may become paranoid as well. It's up to you: Eyes open or eyes closed.

The shit is out there if you're willing to look and face the harsh realities. There was always a hidden agenda; always another layer to the story. The more you dug, the uglier life became. It was up to you how much you could handle. Everything was related in the inner city;

people were incredibly intertwined in each other's lives. You could find out anything if you just took the time. How far down the rabbit hole you decided to go was up to you.

CHAPTER ONE
LANDED ON BLACK

I WAS WORKING A SATURDAY afternoon shift and headed to a neighborhood dispute on the west side. Saturdays were rough on me; I did a double shift on Friday working at one of my many part-time jobs, and then headed straight in for a midnight shift at the police department. I would get off Saturday morning after being relieved by day shift and be back in time to relieve them that afternoon. I did this every Saturday for years. This particular Saturday I had picked up a reserve officer who had ridden with me many times. I liked him. His name was Jeff, and I've mentioned him in my books before; he was smart, thought things through, and never made stupid comments.

We were headed to a neighborhood disturbance, and I was really tired. We arrived at the location and found two families out in the street in a yelling match. I got out and went into mediator mode, listening to both sides and trying to figure out how to diffuse the situation.

The two families had been at each other for months, picking at each other's kids. The kids got into fights with each other, and the parents got into yelling matches over the fights. One family had a dog that barked. Of course, the other family hated the barking dog and complained constantly about it. This is the side of being a cop that never ends up in the crime dramas on television; real life in uniform is not glamorous.

You spend an amazing amount of time reminding grown-ups that they need to remember to act grown-up.

We always had one goal in solving these disputes. Psychologically speaking, the people involved had invariably fallen into thinking in either a "child" or "parent" role. Nothing ever gets resolved when people fall into these mindsets. One party lectures the other, or appears to have the upper hand in the dispute, or—worst case scenario—both parties, no matter what their ages, act like children, and expect the police to arrive and assume the "parent" role and resolve their dispute. Our goal was always to get each side of the dispute to walk willingly into the "adult" role. To talk to each other like adults and resolve the dispute themselves, while we stood by to guide them through the process. Some people did not walk willingly into the "adult" role and had to be dragged, kicking and screaming, into adulthood.

This time, I had the two families calmed down to the point where each would talk civilly to the other, and we were headed toward what I hoped would be a peaceful resolution to the dispute. Maybe, just maybe, I would not be called back around midnight when the beer had been replaced with whiskey and tempers exploded, triggered by the barking dog, or some ridiculous perceived insult to the other family's pride or honor. I could hope, right?

As I was talking to each family, encouraging "adult" role thinking, I could see a man come out of a house across the street. He was slightly overweight, wearing a cowboy hat and cowboy boots, and his potbelly was straining the buttons on his western shirt. He had a large oval belt buckle on his belt that was a sure sign he was a legitimate cowboy, and not a poser, wannabe dime-store cowboy. He had a beer in his hand and from the way he walked and acted, I could see that he was some-what intoxicated and probably had been drinking since the early morning. He stopped and watched the dispute I was trying to resolve, and I hoped that he was smart enough to remain on his porch.

Unfortunately, he was not. He started across the lawn, walking with a swagger that could only be the result of the consistent consumption of alcohol. He was positive he had something to contribute to the discussion that would surely be of great value. I pointed him out to Jeff, my reserve-officer, and asked him to intercept the intoxicated rocket scientist. Jeff did his best to deal with the drunken and self-assured *charro*, while I encouraged the continued de-escalation of the dispute.

Jeff had pretty much convinced the drunk to leave, and things were going well, when the cowboy had an epiphany, turned around, and walked right up to me. Breathing rancid shit-smelling breath in my face, he smiled and proceeded to tell me that I was not nearly as smart as I fucking thought I was, and that he could kick my ass right in front of these people. Then he bumped me with his fat gut. I could see from the two families' reactions to the man that they were afraid of him and were uncomfortable with his presence, and I was pretty sure from their reactions that he was the neighborhood bully and drunk.

What happened next happened so fast that even I was surprised. I drove my right hand up under his jaw, forming a V-shape with my thumb and fingers. I continued to drive him backward until he fell and landed hard on his back. I rolled him over and handcuffed him, arresting him for intoxication and disorderly conduct. Five seconds and done—down, cuffed, and subdued. While I was helping him get up, I may have mentioned to him that he needed to brush his fucking teeth or quit eating his own shit, and that the next time he wanted to kick my ass he should at least bring his fucking "A" game.

I told Jeff to get the car door open, and I placed Mister Shit Breath in the car. I was pissed off now and yelling at Jeff to get in the fucking car. The mediation was on hold, and I told the two families as calmly as I could that I would be back in 20 minutes, the time it would take to book this drunken asshole into jail. They were speechless and wide-eyed, still shocked by how quickly and (admittedly) violently this drunk had been subdued.

While we were taking the guy to jail, I saw Jeff in the backseat watching me carefully. I said to him loudly, "What's up?" He said nothing, just watched me. I let it go and booked the shit-eater into jail. As we were headed back to the neighborhood, Jeff finally started to talk to me.

"Every call with you is an education. I never know what will happen," he said.

"What do you mean?"

"I've watched people spit on you, and you did nothing. I've watched people talk trash to you, call you every name in the book, throw things at you, and I think, *Now he'll get mad and kick some ass* and you don't. Today some drunken guy whispers shit to you and bumps you with his fat gut, and you drop him so fast I could barely see it. I just never know when it will happen."

"When what will happen?" I asked.

"When people will 'land on black' with you. When they land on red, they get to walk away. Even if I think they should have gone to jail, you let them slide. But if they land on black, no matter how slight the insult or crime committed, they are going to jail. You seem to have a switch that gets flipped on, and *bam*! They land on black."

I thought about this and said nothing. I didn't know what the difference was for me. I didn't know what trigger was there, but the shit-eating drunk threatening me and bumping me with his fat gut set it off. I guess Jeff was right; the guy had landed-on-black.

We arrived back at the neighborhood where the dispute had taken place to find that no one was in the street any longer. I went to both families and found that both had a very sudden change of perspective. Each felt there was no need for further talking, and they had mutually agreed that it would be best if they left each other alone and treated each other with respect. This was said to me through locked screen doors as eyes watched me nervously. The same people who just an hour before had been yelling at each other and practically daring each other to fight while I was present were now more than willing to be reasonable.

I smiled. "Okay, but if you need me to come back and help you resolve a dispute, don't be afraid to call before things get out of hand."

Each party agreed, and both quickly closed their doors. I heard deadbolts being thrown in each case as I turned and left. I guess landing on black had its place in neighborhood disputes.

I tried to explain to Jeff what I thought had happened, and he just sat quietly and listened. He brought up several incidents that we had been on together that were much more threatening and dangerous. He was right that I had reacted more calmly during each of them, and had not been angry or aggressive in resolving the incidents. I didn't know what had happened to change that.

Looking back now, I should have recognized this day and this incident as a sign that something *had* changed. This was before the drive-bys, shootings, and gun battles I would become involved in. I was not yet severely damaged, but I was already short-fused and unpredictable. Spit on me and maybe nothing would happen, or maybe something would. I didn't know.

I do know now that there are triggers that set me off. Triggers that throw me into a fight for survival regardless of whether or not there is a real threat. That's the nature of PTSD for me. "Landing on black," describes it most accurately.

To be perfectly clear, there was more to my erratic behavior than just PTSD; the reality of my job was that you could never ever trust that things were as they appeared to be. Minor details would later become crucial to solving cases and bringing the truth to light. People you thought you knew always had hidden agendas. There was always a feint within a feint, and then maybe another one or two more before you reached the rock-bottom truth. Living in that reality, having my life literally depend on being able to recognize a feint for what it was, and digging deeper through the façade all made me edgy as hell and short-tempered. Nothing was ever as it seemed.

CHAPTER TWO
LIFE IS NOT LIKE THE MOVIES

PROSTITUTION IN THE INNER CITY is a fact of life. We would do what we could to keep it at least somewhat subdued. But the reality is it went on all the time, and it was never like what was portrayed in movies. The reality is it is ugly as fuck. Teenage girls barely out of elementary school would be turned out onto the streets by parents to help make ends meet for the family. Older women, lost and alone, with no pension, no money, hungry, and without any skills, would be forced to resort to selling the only thing they had left to sell. It was not pretty; it was survival.

One prostitute I knew was an Indian woman who had lived on the streets for many years. Originally, she had frequented the bars as a younger woman. A lot of people end up hanging out in bars for a period of time, and most move on to some kind of real life. Some, however, do not. They become addicted to the lifestyle. Being known by a bar's patrons, bartender, or owner made them feel accepted, perhaps even important. They end up spending an enormous amount of time at the bar—time and money.

This woman had a name that we all knew her by. I never found out if it was her real name or a nickname. It sounded Indian, so I assumed it was in some way her legitimate name. She went by Laylawetchie, which thinking back, I realize might have been Layla Wetchie. I don't know which is correct. I do know that she lived a life that would make most people sick to their stomachs.

When I first ran into Laylawetchie, we had a report of a dead body in a Dumpster. I got the call and headed to the part of the city that housed most of the lowlife bars. The caller who had reported the body wished to remain anonymous and hung up before the dispatcher could get their information. I signed out on the radio that I was on "the street," as we called the bar district, and started checking Dumpsters for the body, hoping like hell I would not find one. Third Dumpster I checked, I lifted the hard plastic lid, and there was a smell that's impossible to relate. Imagine vomit, rotten food, shit, piss, and the smell of a human body that had not been washed in some time. Here were Laylawetchie and a transient male passed out after having fucked in the Dumpster. That was her thing, fucking in Dumpsters. When she could afford a room for a day or two, she would rent one. Usually, though, she went Dumpster-to-Dumpster, gave blow jobs, and fucked transient and homeless men for a dollar or two. Her personal hygiene was less-than-tolerable.

I woke them up and they both pulled some of their clothing back on. The scene was not pretty—the bodily fluids oozing out of them and the smell of their unwashed bodies, combined with the garbage, made me wretch. They eventually climbed out of the Dumpster, and I sent them on their way. Usually I would check them for warrants, making sure that they were not wanted for some crime, but not today. The smell was over-powering, and it was all I could do to be somewhat respectful.

I informed them that this was not the place to sleep (leaving out the obvious fact that they had been having sex in a Dumpster) and to move along. They moved along, but not before Laylawetchie made a point of offering me a blow job "on the house" because I was "so pretty." She came close enough when she made this "offer" that I was given the full blast of her rancid breath. She had rotten teeth, bleeding gums, and a stench so strong I swear you could actually see her breath. She smiled, trying to regain some dignity after I refused her kind offer. She said I did not know what I was missing out on as she was "the best." Everyone had told her so. I said maybe next time and sent her on her way.

I watched as the two transients made their way down the street, waving their arms and talking to each other about where to go next. That was pretty much her life—Dumpster fucking and blow jobs in any dark corner that would provide the space for her to make a buck or two. You would think that she could not survive long like this, but she was remarkably resilient. She was as much a fixture in the inner city as we were. She was never murdered, or even beaten up too badly. She had been robbed occasionally, but somehow always managed to survive the brutal and demeaning life she'd ended up living.

One night we got a call from the garbage men picking up trash on "the street." They had heard yelling and screaming when the truck's hydraulics lifted the large Dumpster to the top of the truck and started to dump its contents. They exited the truck after returning the industrial-sized container to the ground. A few seconds later, out climbed Laylawetchie, mad as hell that her slumber had been disturbed. They could not believe it when we arrived and knew the filthy woman by name, telling her to move along and find a safer place to sleep.

I had one contact with her when she was at least partially sober, so I asked, why Dumpsters? She said that they always had food in them to eat, and in the winter, the decomposing trash produced heat. Smiling her rotten-toothed smile, she said they kept her warm, dry, and safe. I would have to guess that she was maybe 45- or 50-years-old at the time, but I don't know. I never cared to find out how old she really was.

The vice unit had been tasked with cleaning up the inner city, and decided to start doing sting operations to capture the men who solicited the streetwalkers in my area. It wasn't going to work, but they tried anyway, and made sure to include the press in their efforts. The stings were much-publicized, but accomplished very little. Several prominent businessmen and church officials were caught, along with a couple of military men, and quite a few illegal aliens who worked at menial labor jobs in the area's factories. Our department used female police officers, who would volunteer for the task, to pose as prostitutes. It was risky; they were alone, wore a wire, and were monitored by officers in a car nearby. The hope was that if anything went "sideways," the backup officers would be there in a moment. I never heard of anything bad happening to any of the women, but the potential was definitely there. Surprisingly, some of the female officers were much better than others at getting "hit on." The results were not what we expected. Less-attractive women were stopped and propositioned much more frequently than ones that were more attractive. Eventually, we learned that it was because the more attractive women were quickly detected as undercover cops, they were too pretty, and obviously part of a set-up.

This was true with one exception. One female officer took this as a challenge and when she was approached by the vice unit, she was ready. She was very pretty and planned on making the most out of her first night on the assignment. She went home and changed into an outfit that she had put together just for this purpose. She returned with ratty hair, no makeup, and cut-off shorts that were way too short. She wore a ratty T-shirt that had a hole or two, and hiking boots that were old and worn. She said she had bought them from a secondhand store as the briefing for the operation went on. The transformation was remarkable. Braless and clearly not wearing panties, she hit the street, walking and talking the part. The results were remarkable: she netted more arrests in a two-hour period than any of the other stings combined. She looked the part so well that while vice detectives were removing suspects who had solicited her from one car, another car pulled up and two guys jumped out (right in front of the marked cop cars) and started asking her how much it would cost them for her to fuck both of them. It was hilarious and sad at the same time.

The night wore on and a record number of arrests were made. The real shock for me, though, would occur later at the debriefing held after the operation was over. The female officer said that while she walked the streets pretending to be a hooker, other prostitutes would warn her that there were undercover cops out and that they had inside information that a sting was going to be run that night. It was always interesting to me how quickly our "protected" information made it to the street.

After all the stats were compiled, the press was given the information to publish in the next day's newspapers.

I was walking through the hallway, getting ready to go home. The female officer who'd been so successful in the sting was in an office doing paperwork and talking to her sister on the phone. She had called her sister and asked her to bring over some clothes while she completed paperwork. The two women were talking about the experience and were actually quite excited. I overheard the undercover cop tell her sister that this was an amazing experience. She said never had she felt so wanted sexually in such a blatant and animalistic way. She admitted that it had really "turned her on" and that she now understood how being a "hooker" could be addictive. The two women giggled like little kids and whispered to each other about what had happened during the night. I expected that she would feel revulsion at the various sex acts she had been asked to perform; instead, she liked the idea. I shook my head, amazed at what I was hearing, and left the station.

A week had gone by since the very successful prostitution sting, and I was called to an apartment building in the inner city. A man had called and complained that while he was delivering pizza to an apartment, the occupants had stolen his wallet. That seemed unlikely; usually people who robbed pizza delivery men would wait until the guys had been paid and were leaving the building, then attack, beat, and rob them. This guy claimed to have been robbed inside the apartment by the people who ordered the pizza.

I arrived at a three-story building that had seen much better days. The interior hallways were filthy and littered with trash, and stains on the faded and aging carpet gave indications of why the air smelled like piss and vomit. I was always amazed that the building never had a vacancy for more than a day or two. The slumlord who owned it never had any problem filling vacancies. Before I made my way to the apartment where the complaint came from, I listened in the hallway for a moment. Silence; nothing to indicate that a robbery had occurred—no one yelling, no loud voices, nothing breaking. Quietly I made my way down the hallway to the apartment. A white guy in his mid-20s stood in the hallway, waiting for me. He wore Levis, a button-up shirt, and brown casual shoes. Nothing about him suggested that he was a pizza deliveryman. I asked if he had called, and he said that he had. He said that he had delivered pizza to the apartment, and that they had taken his wallet when he tried to make change for their payment. He did not want to get into trouble, so he'd called the cops. I took down his name and information and asked which restaurant he delivered pizza for. He paused and then told me that he delivered for a new restaurant and told me the name.

I said, "Okay, wait here while I talk to the occupants."

I went to the door of the apartment and knocked. I heard footsteps from the other side, and then a female voice with a Hispanic accent asked, "Who the fuck is it?"

"Police," I said. "Open the door."

Surprisingly, she did so immediately, and told me to come in, walking away from me into the apartment. After a few steps, she turned, and I immediately recognized her. She was missing her right eye, and the flesh on the right side of her face hung loosely on the bone. She had been a drug addict for years, and had suffered a stroke, which had left the right side of her face basically dead to any muscular activity. The flesh hung lifeless and unmoving. The right side of her body had also been affected by the stroke, but not as severely. She was able to walk, and had some movement in her right arm. She was always angry every time we met. Her name was Peta Cruz. Peta was a prostitute, but would refuse to have sex with men. The only sexual service she would provide was a blow job. She did this because she was terrified of getting AIDS and felt that if she only gave blow jobs, that she would not get the disease. She was adamant about it. The picture immediately became crystal-clear. I asked about the pizza story, and Peta replied, "Do I look like I can afford to order a fucking pizza? Since you assholes are trying to arrest us and run us out of the city, we had to get an apartment."

Three women had banded together and rented the apartment, pooling their money. They had their patrons, normally serviced in back alleys and front seats of cars, come to the apartment for blow jobs. That way they were far less likely to be arrested. They were fighting for survival and making do the only way they knew how. It is pretty damn bleak when you realize how harshly some people live, barely surviving, right under your nose. I asked Peta what had happened, and she told me this guy was a regular of hers. Tonight he had come for his usual blow job and had wanted intercourse. She would not allow that, so he refused to pay her. She, in turn, took his wallet and then forced him out of the apartment. I asked her for the wallet and she handed it over freely.

"I assume you have your money."

She said that she did. I asked, "Did you take more than you had agreed to in the deal?" She got mad and threw two twenties at me and said, "Tell that little bitch he'd better never come back." I took the money and the wallet and went out to confront the "pizza deliveryman."

I handed the guy his wallet and money and asked him to make sure that all his money was there. I knew it would be, and after a quick check, he agreed. I said, "Okay, so let's have a coming-to-Jesus talk." I explained the implausibility of the claims he had made about the pizza delivery robbery and asked again the name of the company he worked for. He told me the name of the restaurant, but it was completely different from the original name he had given me. I let him talk and dig himself deeper into the hole he was in.

Finally, I said, "Do you read the newspapers?" When he said he did, I told him he was going to be in them. "I am about to arrest you for solicitation of a prostitute, and when I do, Peta is going to be arrested, too. Do you really want everyone you know to see your picture and Peta's picture in the newspaper? Do you really want your friends to see that you picked up a one-eyed whore who had a stroke and that the right side of her face is dead? Do you want them to know that's what it takes to get you off? Really? Think quickly, fuckhead, because I am running out of patience."

He decided it was time to leave and walked quickly from the apartment building, never looking back. I followed him as he walked, hanging about a block back in my patrol car for nearly a mile until he returned to his own apartment. Strange how he delivered pizza on foot and from his apartment.

CHAPTER THREE

RULE-BREAKER

WHEN I WAS GOING THROUGH FTO (field training), I had to spend two glorious weeks riding with the traffic units. I hated traffic. I mean I really hated it. Writing tickets to mom and pop citizens for speeding and to old ladies for not using their turn signals was just not what I signed up for. I know there is a reason and a purpose for traffic enforcement; I just don't like doing it at all. I would go home feeling like a dick after each day of "enforcement" and counted the days on the calendar until I would finally be done with the traffic enforcement phase of training. I could not wait to get back into a patrol car, answering calls, and hopefully not ruining tax-paying senior citizens' days because they "violated the law."

One day I was sitting at a stop sign, timing each car that stopped, waiting for what we referred to as a "California stop." That was when the driver slowed down to a crawl but never came to a complete stop at the sign. That was a ticket regardless of whether you could see that the driver had looked both ways and could judge whether it was safe to proceed or not. The "letter of the law" said come to a complete stop. The anal traffic guru who mentored me made it clear that we were ridding the world of evil one rolling stop at a time, and this was serious business. In my head I was calling him every fucked-up name I could think of, screaming that I could not wait to get away from his anal-retentive ass, that this candy-ass shit was driving me crazy. On the outside, I smiled and nodded my head. "Yes, yes—we are ridding the world of evil." I had just seven more days to go.

While we sat watching the stop sign, a stabbing was dispatched across the handheld radio. The call was less than a mile away. We were close, and I was jonesing to do something that would make it possible for me to go home and not feel like a complete and total dick. I suggested that we go and help out. The bad guy was reported to still be in the area, covered in blood, and carrying a large knife. He had pretty much gutted another man in a local bar and left on foot. I felt like a racehorse sitting at the starting line, just waiting for some sign that I could explode out of the starting blocks. Seriously—every muscle twitched. I tried to stay calm, but calls like this knifing never came in during the daytime. I waited for the training officer to weigh his options. Finally, after what felt like 10-15 minutes but was probably more like four to five seconds, he said, "Yeah, okay—we can go and search the area, but that's it; we won't be taking statements. And stay away from the actual scene; search the area only. Do you understand?"

I understood. As soon as I heard "yeah," I started the car, and by the time he said "search," the car was in drive and moving forward as fast as I could go. I had a smile on my face for the first time in several days. "Captain Anal" Traffic Enforcement said, "Whoa—hold on! Drive safely, trainee. This is too fast."

I was maybe five mph over the speed limit. I was sure this guy had sex with the lights off and only on the third Wednesday of the month; he was terrified of everything not in the rulebook. I slowed down to the posted limit and crawled to the area of the stabbing. It killed me, but I did not want to be punished for being too dangerous and possibly have to spend a few extra days with Captain Anal.

We searched the area for about ten minutes, but it seemed the bad guy had just disappeared. He was reported to be six feet four inches tall and covered in blood. He had spilled the intestines of the victim out all over the floor of the bar and then left the building; cops were in the area within seconds of the call coming in.

I started to go down a one-way street the wrong way. Captain Anal popped a hemorrhoid right there in the front seat, screaming that this was against the law, and what the hell did I think I was doing? I had to go around the block and enter the area correctly—the entire time being lectured by him about not taking unnecessary risks. I turned down the one-way street from the proper direction of travel and noticed a fire escape that allowed access to the back of a twenty-five-story building that had been vacant for years in the middle of the city. I thought to myself, "That's where I would go."

I pulled into the building's rear parking lot, stopped, and got out. Captain Anal said, "Where you going, trainee?"

"Let's check the area around this building. Maybe he hit the fire escape and found an open door."

We walked around the building and found nothing. I started up the fire escape, and by the fifth floor Captain Anal was breathing heavily. I could see that ten, maybe twelve floors up, the door had been pried open and was slightly ajar. By the time we got that high, Captain Anal was in pending cardiac arrest.

I opened the door and looked inside the pitch-dark building. The Captain had enough by that point. He said, "No way in hell we are going in there, rookie! There are old cops and there are bold cops, but there are no old bold cops. I plan on being an old cop. Turn around now. We are not going in there."

I could not believe it. On the outside, I said, "Okay, sure." On the inside I was taunting him, calling him chickenshit and saying that he had no business training anyone. We walked down the stairs and left the area, returning to the stop sign, listening to the patrol units still searching the area.

For years, I would walk up that fire escape and enter the building through the door that had been pried open. I searched the building top to bottom several times in the middle of the night, with no backup. Using low light and walking quietly, I surprised dozens of people hiding out in the dark inside the abandoned building. Some lit fires and would "camp" inside the building during the winters. I found a surprising number of people with outstanding warrants and made several arrests by searching the building on a regular basis. I never did find the guy who did the stabbing while I was riding with Captain Anal. He was eventually caught, however, and later admitted he was in the building and heard us coming up the fire escape. I will never know what would have happened if we had searched for him. I do know that I hated being afraid of anyone or anything, regardless of the situation. I never wanted to walk away from a dark building just because I did not have the confidence to enter it. I would enter it and knew I would overcome whatever was inside. No matter what the circumstances, I would be more prepared than the guy in the dark with a knife listening to me coming up the fire escape for him. I was prepared. He had better fear me.

That call made me determined not to walk away just because things got a little dicey. I wanted to be really familiar with everything in my area—every nook and cranny, every alleyway, every dark parking lot. There were several privately owned parking terraces that drug dealers and prostitutes used to conduct business after the daywalkers had gone home. Because there was no obvious way into these structures for the "rule followers," the drug dealers felt they were safe. Smiling, I would enter the outbound lanes. I kept duct tape in the trunk of my car and would tape the tire rippers that were everywhere on the privately owned parking terraces' exit lanes, then I would roar into the lot, going in via the outbound lanes, watching the night people scatter as I drove in. I was breaking the rules and going against the grain, seeing things with new eyes, and digging deeper. Waiting for the next landed-on-black moment.

CHAPTER FOUR

TRUST NO ONE, TRUST NOTHING

IT IS PROBABLY OBVIOUS BY now I have learned to trust no one. A lifetime of being lied to, betrayed, and manipulated can make you that way. I've always felt everyone had an agenda behind the scenes; it was just a matter of being smart enough and alert enough to figure it out.

When I was on the SWAT team, we were the first in our area to be allowed to carry the latest technology in less-than-lethal force, pepper spray. Being able to carry the spray was supposed to be a privilege to us as cops and SWAT team members, because it would give us another tool in our arsenal, hopefully making the job less dangerous for us.

The problem with this privilege was that to be able to carry it, we had to agree to be sprayed with it. No choice; if you wanted to be on SWAT, you had to be sprayed. I later realized there were many reasons for this. First, we needed to know the incredible pain that we would be subjecting people to. Personally, this made me less likely to use it; the pain was incredible, and we referred to the spray as "liquid fire" after our training.

Some guys used it frequently, and one guy we worked with even earned the nickname "Rainbird" because he used it so damn often. We used to joke that he started off each traffic stop, each field interview, and every call he went on with his pepper spray out and pointed in the face of the person he was in contact with, looking for a reason to spray him or her. It was ridiculous how often he sprayed people. Three years after the initial training, I still had a nearly full can of pepper spray, while he was on his fifth can. Suspicious? You decide.

Finally the day came that we were to be sprayed, we were nervous, and rightly so. Paramedics and the fire department were standing by to treat us. We lined up and, one by one, had to look straight ahead, eyes open, and be sprayed in the face. I later realized the second benefit to the training was to provide the paramedics with human guinea pigs to practice treatment options. They were learning how to properly treat the suspects we would be spraying.

The entire training day was videotaped, and we were told it would be kept if needed to demonstrate in court that we were properly trained. I thought nothing of it.

A few months passed, and a friend of mine was teaching in the police academy. He asked me to take a ride-along with a cadet from the academy. He knew that I did not like ride-alongs, but he claimed this cadet was "very squared away," and he would vouch for her trustworthiness. At the time, I trusted him; he was in the gang unit, and we had been on SWAT together. He was very direct and blunt. On the streets, the gang members called him Robo—as in Robocop. He was cool as hell under pressure. I agreed to take the ride-along, and by the time the night was over, I was unimpressed.

I did not know what he saw in her, but she was definitely not "squared away." To start with, she had a haircut that made her look like a hedgehog. More importantly, she was a giggly mess, and all she talked about was the "cool pepper spray video" that Robo had shown at the academy. I felt like I was on a blind date and had been blindsided by Robo. It quickly became obvious that she had become infatuated with me after watching the video. It was weird as hell—she knew everything I had said and done on the video; she'd basically memorized the whole thing. Finally, she admitted that Robo had made her a copy of the video and that she watched it a lot at home. This was creepy shit. When the shift was over, she asked if she could ride with me again, and I told her she would have to go through Robo. Would I give her my number? No. She walked away disappointed and rejected.

Later that week, Robo got a hold of me and asked for feedback. I said nothing about the video and just said that it went fine, no worries. When he asked if she could ride with me again, I said it would be better for a new cadet to get a variety of ride-along experiences and not just ride with someone as jaded as I was. He was silent and watched me for some hint of what this really meant. I gave nothing away, so he said that I was probably right and that he would consider it. I saw the Hedgehog out on a ride-along with several different officers after that. I felt that maybe the crush was over with and I relaxed a bit.

One night, Robo called me and asked for a favor. I told him to name it. He said, "Do you remember that ride-along I had you take out from the academy?" I said I did; Hedgehog was burned into my mind, as creepy as fuck, and on my always-avoid list. He said that she had an ex-husband who had been stalking her, and she had called Robo to report that she thought he had broken into her condo. She asked Robo to come take the report, but he felt it was a conflict of interest and asked me to take the call. I agreed. Robo gave me her address, and I went to the condo.

When I got there and knocked on the door, Hedgehog was waiting—candles lit, incense burning. Silky short-shorts and a sheer camisole were all she wore. She greeted me and asked me to come in. I walked into the condo and saw, once again, I had been setup. In the back of my mind, I could hear the robot from the television series *Lost in Space* calling, "Danger, Will Robinson, danger!"

Hedgehog tried to make small talk, asking me about how the night had been going as she sipped a glass of red wine. I told her Robo said she had reported that her condo had been broken into. She stopped suddenly and said, "Oh! Yes!"

The lights came on, and she threw on a robe and started to try to lie her way through a bullshit account of an attempted burglary. By the time she was done, psycho Hedgehog had worked herself into a crying, snot-dripping mess. There were no signs that anything she claimed had actually happened. I told her that I could put an extra patrol on her condo, and she thanked me. She said knowing I would be conducting an extra patrol made her feel safer. I explained I would not be doing it personally, as she did not live in my area. I had taken the call as a favor to Robo. That was the only reason I was there. She said, "Oh. Okay."

I left and put the extra patrol on the address. Robo called me on the radio a few minutes later and asked me to call him in his office. I explained there was no sign of a burglary, and that Hedgehog was a fucking nut. I told him not to ask me for any more favors where Hedgehog was concerned. He apologized and said that he had no idea she was interested in me at all; he was just trying to help her out. Yeah, right. Regardless, he never asked me to do anything for him or the Hedgehog again.

A few years later, I got a call from one of the dispatchers I'd been friends with for years. Her name was Maggie. We were always very direct with each other, and she got right to the point.

"Have you lost your fucking mind?" she asked.

I was stunned and asked her what she meant.

She said, "You know what the hell I mean. Are you really that hard up that you would fuck Kristie?"

I had no idea what she was talking about. "Who the hell is Kristie?"

"Don't play stupid with me, you asshole. I know that you're seeing Kristie. She's telling everyone that you two have been having an affair for two years now and that you are leaving your wife for her. Of all the women who have thrown themselves at you—you chose to fuck *Kristie*? Are you really that sick in the fucking head? She is *gross*! What is wrong with you? Jesus!"

For a moment, I was speechless. Then I said, "Maggie, is this another one of your pranks?" We constantly pulled pranks on each other and sometimes the pranks were amazingly elaborate. So I never knew what to expect from her.

She said, "I wish it was a prank. I'm sick to my stomach up here in dispatch listening to her brag about the last weekend you spent with her at the cabin you rented in the woods. She goes on and on about the amazing sex that you had, and how you just can't get enough of her."

I listened, thinking that this was too elaborate even for Maggie. She was really angry. So I decided to call her bluff—if it was one.

"Maggie, I don't even know anyone named Kristie. Does she work with you?"

"Yes," Maggie said. "She's here right now."

"Okay—I'm on my way. Don't say anything to anyone. I'll knock and come in, and you can see for yourself. Let Kristie answer the door when I knock."

I signed out, saying that I was available for urgent calls only, then headed to dispatch. I got out of my car and knocked on the door. A few seconds later the door opened, and guess who answered it? Hedgehog.

The look on her face was priceless. She did not say a word as I walked past her to Maggie's dispatch console. I sat down and said to Maggie, "Jesus! No wonder you're so mad. Now I get it!"

Maggie said, "Okay—I can tell now by her reaction to you that you're telling the truth. She's terrified!"

We talked quietly for about a half hour while I told her about the academy video, ride-along, and fake burglary/bootie call she and Robo had used to set me up. I said I didn't know who she was having an affair with, but it was not me. Maggie apologized and said she would try to find out who it was Hedgehog was really seeing.

About a month passed, and Maggie called me to tell me that Hedgehog had finally caved in and told the truth. She was fucking a deputy sheriff and had told everyone she was fucking me to keep the heat off him. Lucky me. Thank God, Maggie called me so I knew what was going on.

At about the same time, my brother had been dating a records clerk in the police department. He was a cop, too, and they had been dating for some time. Eventually she became pregnant. I didn't like her at all, and I could not see what my brother saw in her. I made that painfully clear every time I saw her: *You might be his girlfriend/ baby-momma, but we are not friends or family.* It was painfully obvious to her that I would have nothing to do with her. She was about as sick and bent as she could possibly be. She was a constant drama queen and told people frequently that my brother beat her and abused her. I seriously doubted that. They had their disagreements, but I know he never laid a hand on her; we were both cops, and that kind of thing was a career-ending mistake for a cop. I tried to talk to him about the claims of abuse and he said, "Oh, that's just her weird sense of humor. Just blow it off."

Their baby was born, and things seemed to settle down; the bullshit stories of abuse and beatings stopped. Her need for attention was too extreme for this peace and quiet to last for long, though.

I came to work one day and one of the secretaries I liked pulled me aside and said, "Really—you and Emily?"

I said, "Me and Emily what?"

She stared at me and said, "I should have known you would never touch that nasty skank."

I was lost in this conversation and asked her what the hell she was talking about. She told me that my brother's baby-momma was telling everyone in the department that she had no idea who the father of her baby was—HIM OR ME!

I knew I could trust this secretary, probably more than I could trust anyone else in the department. So I knew she was serious when she told me that Emily was telling everyone this bullshit. I was furious. What kind of sick fuck jokes about this kind of shit—much less goes around straight-faced and tells everyone lies like this just to get attention? I had to go to shift briefing, and when it was finished, I came out and jumped on the radio and called my brother, asking for a meeting.

When I saw him, I explained what I had been told, not telling him who had told me. He laughed and said, "I told you she has a weird sense of humor. Just ignore it. It's no big deal."

I made it clear that I did not appreciate this sick shit. People in the department believed these rumors, and he might not care, but I did. My brother said that I needed to relax and to learn not to put so much weight in other people's opinions. He drove off, leaving me there fuming. My kids were sacred to me, all of them; he had kids strewn all over hell and did not take care of any of them, so the thought of people wondering whether or not he was the father of this child did not bother him at all.

Like I've said before, karma is an evil bitch with a very long memory. Evidently, this time at least, karma was on my side. I had been fucked with to no end at this point, and trusted no one but a very small circle of cops and one secretary. Robo was not part of the circle of people I trusted, nor were many others.

One day, nearly a year later, I came to work and sat quietly at the back of the room during briefing. In the middle of briefing, a few of the guys who had been hired around the same time as my brother turned and said, "Wow, you Fortier boys sure do have interesting lives!"

I was instantly angry at being lumped in with my brother; we were not the same kind of cop. I had made a lifetime out of trying to prove I was related only by blood, not by action. (There were many times I seriously doubted we were related at all, but that's another story.) I tried to curb my obvious rage at being compared to my brother and asked, as calmly as possible, what they meant. The loudest of the group said that it was common knowledge that my brother's baby-momma had been telling everyone that she had no idea who the real father of her child was, him or me.

I sighed deeply and replied that I would no more fuck that nasty bitch than fuck Ellen. Ellen was a 350-pound monster of a woman who worked in records with Emily. She had no hair and few teeth, and smelled awful. They all laughed at that; no one could doubt I was serious. I never minced words when it came to my brother or his choice of women.

The loudmouth cop said, "Okay, okay—I believe you. But you might want to pass on to your brother that he needs to be aware that Emily is telling everyone that he won't have sex with her and that he has gone to the dark side."

I said, "The dark side?"

"Yeah, she says your brother is gay, and has been watching gay porn and has been buying gay porn magazines."

"Really?" I said.

He laughed and said that she had been spreading this shit for the past month. I smiled and thanked him.

I left briefing with a smile on my face for the first time in a long time. Personally, I couldn't care less what anyone's sexual preferences are. Looking at Emily as we passed in the hallway, I thought seriously that I would almost rather be gay than go there. She was awful. What my brother saw in her I will never know.

I drove around for a couple of hours and finally called my brother for a meeting. We met in a cemetery, cars pulled up side-by-side, inches from each other's car doors. I started to build the story carefully, telling him that I had come to work tired today and in no mood to take anyone's bullshit in briefing. I said that the other guys in briefing had mentioned that Emily was still telling everyone that she had no idea whether the real father of their baby was HIM or ME. I laughed a fake laugh and said, "I finally get it, though—she has a hilarious sense of humor."

He smiled and said, "I'm glad you calmed down about this. It's no big deal. Who cares what these bozos think?"

I laughed again and told him I agreed. "It's probably hilarious to you what she's telling everyone lately right?" I asked.

He smiled an uneasy smile and sort of laughed and said, "What's that?"

"She's telling everyone that you're gay. She says she came home and found you masturbating to gay porn, and she has found several gay men's magazines around the house." I embellished on the masturbation part, but it was payback time.

The grin fell off his face, and my hugely homophobic brother was instantly filled with fear and terror. He said, "Are you shitting me? You are fucking shitting me, right?"

I laughed and said, "No, but don't worry—it's just her weird sense of humor."

He was furious. "Tell me what they told you exactly, word for word."

I told him everything they said, and added in the masturbation scene for good measure. Then I said, "But it's like you said—we shouldn't give a shit what these people think, right? I mean, it's just her sense of humor, and who does it hurt anyway?" Then I laughed another hard, fake laugh.

He could not get his car started fast enough. The engine roared to life as he sped out of the cemetery and picked up the radio angrily to demand a meeting with his baby-momma. She had recently been promoted out of records, and was out on the streets with a radio, riding around in a meter-maid golf cart.

I heard that their conversation was not pretty. I guess he did not appreciate her sense of humor anymore. I, however, enjoyed the rest of that shift immensely. What goes around had finally come back around. And this time, at least, I was able to enjoy it for a moment.

CHAPTER FIVE

PERSPECTIVE IS EVERYTHING

NOT TOO LONG AGO, THERE was a lot of speculation in the news about a particular case that happened on the East Coast. People were extremely polarized in their opinions of what happened that night. One guy who was Hispanic called the cops to report another guy who he thought was behaving suspiciously.

The alleged suspect was a black male. The police dispatcher told the caller to stay put and not confront the other man. The caller did not do as he was told; he confronted the man, and a fight broke out. In the end, the black guy was killed. I was not there, and I have no idea what happened. I don't pretend to know. I do know that we dealt with citizens all the time who were overzealous and would turn a simple misunderstanding into a shit storm.

Just as in this case, the uninitiated and untrained would have no idea what they were getting into and, due to their lack of experience and knowledge, the problem would escalate instead of de-escalating. Race became an issue in this particular case, and even the President weighed in to say that he, too, had been treated differently because of his race until he became a Senator. I don't pretend to know what life was like for others. I would never know what it meant to be a black man or woman in this country. I did get a glimpse of what it might be like one day, and it was an eye-opening experience.

Here's what happened. You decide for yourself what to think.

I got a call to respond to one of the city's malls on a disturbance. There was a report from mall security that an assistant manager at a store that sold costume jewelry had stopped a woman. The store was on the second floor of the mall located at the far end. It was a very popular shop among younger women and their daughters, and had a significant problem with shoplifting.

When I arrived at the mall, I parked in a loading area and entered through a service area in the middle of the mall. As soon as I entered the mall, I heard yelling—and not just yelling, but enraged screaming and wailing. There was no doubt that a disturbance was definitely going on. I walked to the area where the screaming came from and contacted the mall security guard. He was a friend and normally pretty animated, always joking. We spent a lot of time together and got along very well. This time, however, he was serious and sullen.

He said the clerk had called him to the store because she felt threatened by a woman. She had been following her because she thought she was a shoplifter. When he arrived, he found the clerk had stopped a black woman and her children. He said that he had been able to calm her down at first, primarily because she trusted him because he was also black. The woman identified herself as Deborah Jones. She told him that she had come to the mall with her children, and her three small girls wanted to go to the shop because it was their favorite place. They loved the brightly colored costume jewelry, and it was sold at a price they could afford. Deborah said the girls were starting school the following week and wanted to have some new jewelry to wear the first day.

While they were shopping, Deborah said the clerk asked if they needed any help. She thanked the clerk and said they were fine. Instead of leaving, the clerk remained next to them, watching everything they did, and it was obvious the clerk was suspicious. Deborah said she felt threatened by the blatant and accusatory manner of the clerk. She asked the clerk why she was still there when she had stated she didn't require any assistance.

The clerk said she knew that Deborah was in the store to steal jewelry, and that she would not leave her unobserved as long as she was there. Deborah said she was shocked at the bold comment and had replied, "What makes you think me or my children are stealing?" Deborah then told the mall security guard "the fucking bitch clerk told me she knew that we would steal because we are black." Deborah said she lost her temper at that comment and started yelling, which frightened the clerk, who then called security.

I asked the security guard what he thought about the clerk. He said, "Man, I don't know. I talk to the clerk all the time, and she seems friendly enough. I have never got that vibe from her; it's hard for me to believe."

"So what set Deborah off again? You told me you had her calmed down, and she had given you all this information. She's losing her mind now, so what happened?"

He replied, "I told her I would have to call the police and that I could not resolve this without police intervention. When she heard that, she lost it and started screaming."

I watched the hysterical woman for a moment and then looked at her girls. They were in tears, terrified at their mother's crazed, emotional ranting and my appearance on the scene. I tried to talk to Deborah and get her to calm down. At that point all I had was a disturbance, no one had to go to jail; I just needed to find a peaceful resolution of the dispute. The more I talked to Deborah, the worse she became—more frantic, threatened, hysterical, and out of control. She started throwing things and swearing. She claimed that the only reason she had been followed was because she was a black woman. She had done nothing wrong, and her daughters had done nothing wrong, and that this was fucking bullshit! I asked her again to lower her voice and talk reasonably with me to get this resolved. She screamed, "Fuck you, motherfucker!"

The mall security guard said, "You're going to have to remove her. I can't have this shit going on in the mall." I arrested her and, after several minutes, she calmed down enough to give me a phone number so that I could call her mother to come get her children. I walked her out of the mall with her screaming and ranting that the only reason she was being arrested was because she was black. When we got to the police car, she freaked out and said, "Now what? Are you gonna beat my ass next?" I put her in the car and sat there, waiting for her to calm down. Finally, after 20 minutes, she just stopped ranting and looked at me and said, "These handcuffs hurt. I want to go home."

Now that she was reasonable, I told her that she probably did not remember me, but we had gone to the same high school. We even had a class together. And I had not arrested her because she was black. I had arrested her because she was out of control and caused a scene at the mall. She was going to jail for disorderly conduct. That was all. I asked her again what had happened, and she recounted the same story that the mall security guard had told me.

"Okay. I'm going to take you to jail now, and I will come back and ask the clerk what happened," I said.

"What the fuck ever, that bitch ain't gonna tell you shit. She isn't that stupid!"

I booked Deborah and came back to the mall and located the clerk. She said she had been working at the store for several years and that she had worked her way up to assistant manager. I asked her what specifically had drawn her attention to Deborah and her girls. She said they came in and started touching everything and that she could just tell they were going to steal. I asked specifically what they had done. The clerk looked at me long and hard, and then pulled up the sleeve on her shirt and rubbed her index and middle fingers up and down on her arm. I asked what that meant. She rolled her eyes and repeated the gesture again in a more urgent manner and shrugged.

I said, "Look, I need verbal responses not gestures."

"Black!" she blurted out. "They are black, they all steal, all black people steal from us all the goddamn time."

I was stunned. I played along momentarily and said, "Oh yeah, okay, I just needed to hear it." I asked for her manager's name and phone number and explained I had arrested Deborah for the scene she had caused but not for anything else.

"Really?" she said. "That was it? She wasn't wanted by the police for anything?"

"No. What made you think she would be?"

She smiled at me and whispered, "Duh…they're all criminals. You know that."

"You mean black people?"

"Of course!" she said.

"You know what? I see a lot of weird shit in this job, I really do. Today, though, you made it to the top of my 'weird shit' list." I leaned in and motioned for her to come closer, which she did.

"You," I said quietly, "are a racist bitch, and you make me sick. I am going to call your manager and explain what happened today. When I come back tomorrow if you are still working here, I will contact the mall manager and get this entire fucking store removed from the mall. No one should have to deal with this racist shit."

Her smile disappeared; her face was flushed as she glared at me, fearful now.

I smiled. "Good luck with your new job."

I called the store manager from my car and detailed the incident. I explained in very clear language that I would be watching the store from now on, and if I saw continued profiling of their customers like this, there would be serious consequences. The manager said the assistant manager would be fired immediately. I said I was still at the mall and that immediately meant "right now." I said I would be waiting to see her exit the building.

Twenty minutes later, my friend the mall security guard walked the clerk out and issued her a no-trespass warning. She had not only lost her job, she could not return to the mall—even to shop—ever.

Three months later, I was subpoenaed to appear in court for the Deborah Jones case. I arrived and started to brief the prosecuting attorney on the incident. He was not willing to cut Jones a deal. He wanted to go for the maximum penalty possible. He had read the report and felt her reaction to the clerk was unwarranted.

I said, "Look, man, I went back and talked to the clerk. She was a racist pig. She admitted that she followed Deborah only because she was black."

He did not care and wanted to go forward with the case.

"Okay—put me on the stand. Go ahead. I'll testify about the way I felt after hearing the clerk admit what she'd done. I was really pissed, too. Do you think the judge will be happy that you didn't dismiss this case after he hears the facts? Really? What the fuck is wrong with you?"

He threw the case file on his desk and stormed out of the office. Ten minutes later, Deborah had her case dismissed. The prosecuting attorney was furious and told me to get the hell out of his office. I left the building and met Deborah outside. She came up and hugged me, tears flowing down her face.

"You *did* go back and talk to the clerk! I read the report. She admitted what she'd done." I nodded and told her that if she had just calmed down, I would not have had to arrest her, but I did understand her rage. The clerk had pissed me off as well. From then on, when I drove past Deborah Jones's house in my patrol car, she would wave and smile. She even called me over to meet her three girls one day and explained that I was "mommy's police officer friend" as she hugged me.

CHAPTER SIX

ALWAYS WEAR A HELMET

WORKING PATROL ONE NIGHT, WE got a call about an automobile crash. I hated traffic and anything to do with it. I was not busy, however, and it was a slow night, so I headed toward the crash to help out with traffic control, witness statements, etc. We all did everything we could to help each other out whenever possible. While on my way to the scene, the first officer to arrive came over the radio and announced that there was no hurry for medical, as this was obviously an "Echo." Echo was our radio code for "fatality"; whoever had crashed was already dead.

We never called out a fatal unless it was painfully obvious that there was no miracle life-saving magic capable of bringing this person back to life. That meant the scene was going to be meticulously investigated and, more likely than not, very messy. Just before I arrived, I asked the officer who had been assigned the call where he would like me to setup to assist in traffic control. He directed me to close off one end of an entire block of the busy four-lane street on which the crash had occurred. He wanted all traffic lanes shut down. This was highly unusual. I knew then that the scene must really be bad.

We spent several hours interviewing witnesses and collecting evidence. The department's advanced traffic investigation unit was called in to measure skids and help collect evidence. CSI was called as well to document the scene. The duty lieutenant asked on the radio for an update. The officer in charge of the scene would not answer the request on the radio, and told the lieutenant he would need to come to the scene to see for himself.

I was very busy dealing with the traffic control. If this crash had occurred during normal daylight hours, it would have been a nightmare. Since it was 1:30 in the morning, the traffic was manageable. Anyone who directs traffic against the normal flow will tell you that people are amazingly difficult to deal with under such circumstances. They develop a routine and follow that routine almost daily. Then here you are telling them they have to turn left or right instead of continuing straight, and their brains shut down. Seriously shut down. They look at you, eyes blinking, an empty, brainless gaze meets yours, and they ask, "Well, what am I supposed to do? I've always gone straight here. How do I get home?"

This is a reality check into the problem-solving skills of your fellow citizens that you will experience nowhere else. I would explain to the baffled motorists that they needed to drive one block east, then turn left, drive another block north, and turn left again, and they would be back on their beloved, well-worn path. That all would be as it always had been, and not to worry. I would assure them that their life wouldn't end because they had to go one block out of their way.

You would be amazed at how difficult this is for people to do. I know that it seems ridiculous, and after you've experienced it yourself, you realize just how ridiculous it really is. Herding cattle in a direction they don't want to go feels very similar, in terms of both effort and frustration.

I was busy herding the traffic against the usual flow and wondering why I had volunteered for this task when, finally, a reserve officer relieved me. I wished him luck. I went to help out at the block-long accident scene. I pulled into a parking lot, got out of my patrol car, and walked to the scene. I admit it was kind of mind-boggling. Usually at accident scenes there might be a few evidence markers and markings on the pavement where the accident reconstruction team notes the start of skid marks, the impact, the point of collision, and the final resting point of the vehicles. That was the usual. This was not the usual scene.

It turned out that a bullet bike had been ridden by a guy wearing a helmet, shorts, and a T-shirt. He wore no gloves and no boots. Just a helmet and summer clothes and running shoes. Not even socks. He had been racing a car, and when the race had started, he had left the car in the dust, speeding off easily and defeating the car. Two blocks later, catching the traffic lights as they changed in his favor, he had continued to accelerate. Traffic accident reconstruction showed that he had reached approximately 125 mph when something went wrong. Maybe the bike hit a rock, or a cat or a dog ran into the road. We never knew for sure, but what we did know was that at 125 mph, the bike and the motorcyclist hit the pavement, flipped, and then basically exploded in various parts from the violence of the impact. There were bike parts everywhere, spread in a long, cone-shaped debris field. The bike looked like it had been blown up in an explosion.

The male driver had not fared much better than his motorcycle. We actually had to form a line at the beginning of the scene and walk carefully forward. As we searched for and located body parts, the line would stop and the part would be marked for collection by CSI. A foot here, a finger there; one kneecap was discovered in the gutter. A foot still in its running shoe was found under a parked car. There were bits of flesh and bone strewn along the roadway in what was one of the most horrible scenes I had ever been on.

We walked silently, looking for parts of the guy's body, hoping this task would be finished sooner rather than later. No one wanted to say much; we just had to grit our teeth and get through it. Eventually someone started to mumble about how stupid this guy had been going that fast, and how the idiot had got what he deserved. We all agreed it had been really stupid to go so fast. Then someone yelled out, "But at least he was wearing a helmet, right? I mean, that's what you're told—always wear a helmet!" We all laughed as the reality of that comment hit home. No helmet would keep you alive at those speeds.

Finally, we came across the helmet. We all stood around saying nothing for a moment; finally, someone had the courage to lift the dark visor. Staring back at us was a horrified face, its mouth still frozen in a silent scream, eyes glazed and staring out of the helmet into nothing. There was a pause and then, almost simultaneously, we broke into hysterical laughter. Someone said "Damn good thing you wore a fucking helmet, genius!"

We were instantly transformed, now laughing hysterically, tears rolling down our faces as we called CSI over to the helmet. We could not stop laughing and making harsh, smart-ass remarks about the logic of wearing a helmet at 125 mph. This was how we dealt with the horror of this scene and, like it or not, it did help us cope. The scene was a brutal example of how incredibly fragile life was. One stupid decision and you are being scraped and hosed off the pavement.

Once all the big pieces of both bike and biker were collected, the fire department came in and hosed off the pavement, cleaning up the scene. We could not leave a scene like this for the daywalkers to see. It was much too horrible for the people I had previously been trying to help by directing them to go one block out of their way. For that same reason, the crash was never mentioned in the daily newspaper.

CHAPTER SEVEN

NEVER CRY WOLF

ONE NIGHT, A 16-YEAR-OLD KID was brought into the emergency room by two of his friends. He'd been badly beaten up and was bleeding profusely from his head and face. He said that he had been walking in the central part of the city with his two friends, and that a truck loaded with "white supremacists" pulled over and beat him up because he was a white guy hanging out with his two black friends. He said this white supremacist gang targeted him, calling him a "nigger lover," and then beat him up. He told his friends to run and get help, and that he held off the gang as long as he could, but finally they got the better of him and beat him unconscious. His friends returned to the area after they had called the police. The gang left him bleeding in the parking lot where they had trapped him, and they were gone. His friends brought him to the hospital immediately. The victim suffered a broken jaw and had several broken teeth from the attack. He was admitted to the hospital and was listed in stable condition.

The emergency room called the police department and reported the incident, and the case was immediately assigned to detectives, given the nature of the claims. This was classified as a hate crime, and had huge political and legal implications. A law had recently been passed by state legislature to enable prosecutors to punish hate crimes more vigorously. Detectives started their investigation and interviewed both the witnesses to the incident. They were able to get corroborating statements, and believed the incident happened as reported. The two witnesses said that a 1975–80 model pickup truck, dark blue or black in color, had pulled up and that four white males had jumped out of the truck and beaten up the victim. The suspects were all wearing blue Levis and "wife-beater" T-shirts, and had completely shaved heads.

The detectives went to the scene of the beating—a dark parking lot off a well-traveled street—and found evidence that supported the victim's claims. There were blood splatters on the asphalt and bits of torn clothing that matched the victim. Gang unit detectives were given the lead on the case due to the fact that a white supremacist gang was suspected.

As you can imagine, the case immediately gained the attention of the media in the area. It was a reporter's wet dream. The reporters who covered the case had been in college in the 60s, and this white guy being beaten for associating with his two black friends was exactly the type of story they had gone into journalism to cover. Here was a legitimate hate crime, right in our city, just a few weeks after the new laws had been passed!

The reporters pushed the detectives assigned to the case for details nearly every day. Several press conferences had to be held to appease the media's demands of the city government and police department to prove that they were not brushing the case off and simply going through the motions. The local media had become a self-appointed watchdog to ensure that the "establishment" did not drag its feet in pursuing the racist gang members.

There were several front-page articles about the progress on the case. As you can imagine, it was a nightmare for the detectives assigned to investigate it. Instead of devoting themselves to investigating the case and following leads, they were forced to spend a lot of time briefing city officials and police department administrators. To make matters worse for the detectives, once administration became involved, they suddenly decided that they had valuable insight into how the case should be investigated. They offered friendly suggestions and advice, and then wanted to know the outcome of these suggestions. Were they successful? If not, they had lots of ideas they thought would help. Yep, idiots came crawling out of the woodwork at an alarming rate.

Several weeks passed and there was no break in the case; no arrests had been made. The pressure on the detectives to make an arrest was incredible. In order to appease the media, the police administration made idle threats about replacing the assigned detectives with new ones. This was a common tactic by the administration in our department, which enabled them to point a finger at someone, place blame for a lack of progress, and make themselves look good at the same time. But, the reality was, no one wanted the case. It was a political nightmare. It didn't matter who worked the case—no one would have made any progress. The detectives assigned had left no stone unturned and had followed every lead.

I was working the west end of the city about a month later when I came across a group of gang members drinking beer under a bridge. I called the gang unit out of courtesy to allow them to deal with the case, as a way to build rapport, and so they could document the members of the gang. Our standard procedure at the time was to make them pour out the alcohol, and let them know that they could be arrested for possession of alcohol by a minor. Not tonight, though; they were being cooperative, so I didn't do this. We did this for a reason. We desperately needed informants to find out what was going on within the gangs.

In this instance, the younger gang members were taken home to parents. This enabled us to verify home addresses and where they actually lived, not just where they told us they lived. Eventually, only the senior members of the gang were left, and we sat against the hood of my car, talking to them. The most senior gang member who was present was a man named Leland Afuvi, whom I mentioned in my book, *Street Creds*. We had a good rapport with this gang and they with us. We were definitely antagonists but not enemies. It was understood that we would both kill each other if needed, but we also had a mutual respect for one another. That may sound odd, but it's a fact.

The small talk eventually turned to the case of the beating committed by the white supremacists. Afuvi asked if there was any break in the case, and whether the gang unit had any leads or were just letting the case slide because they were really racist, too. This really pissed off the gang detective, and he quickly replied, "Fuck you, Leland."

Afuvi laughed, knowing that he had got under the detective's skin. He said, "Damn, I was just joking, Detective Rinker. So really, what's the latest on that case? Are you any closer to an arrest?"

Rinker calmed down and repeated, "Fuck you, Leland. And no, I am no closer to arresting the skinheads who beat this guy's ass. I can't find anyone who knows anything about it."

Leland smiled. "Skinheads, huh?"

"Yes. That's what the witnesses said."

Leland laughed again. "Well, good luck, Detective, in finding your suspects. I guess I need to go home now and get a haircut." Leland smiled and rubbed his head as he walked away from us, heading toward home. We didn't think anything of his comment; we just stayed and talked for a few minutes and finally went on to other calls.

About a week went by, and Detective Rinker called me down to the gang unit office. It was late at night, and he had specifically asked dispatchers to send me to the gang office for a meeting. When I arrived I said, "What's up, man?"

"Do you remember that night about a week ago when you called me to the bridge where the gang members were drinking?"

I said I did.

"Do you remember Leland Afuvi asking about the hate crime I've been working for the past couple of months?"

"Yes. Why?"

"I finally got a break in the case."

"No shit?" I said, surprised. "What happened?"

Rinker said he was driving around the city late one night and thinking about a conversation we'd had. I had told him how I thought it was really important to listen to people and let them talk, because I learned more about what was going on by what they didn't say or wouldn't talk about than by what they openly admitted. The streets are always an education, and the more I understood, the more I listened, and then I stopped talking so damned much.

"Do you remember what Leland said about needing a haircut?"

Yes, I did remember the odd comment.

"Well, I was driving around, and it hit me: he was telling us right there that this was not a hate crime. *He* was one of the guys who participated in the beating. It wasn't a hate crime at all! They were jumping the victim into the gang. He'd been beaten up as an initiation, and to cover up the beating to his parents, he came up with this bullshit story."

"So when do you release this to the press?" I asked, amused. "I can't wait to hear what they have to say about this after the way they've been riding your ass about dragging your feet on this 'hate crime'."

"I just got the confession from the victim that he lied about the whole thing, and the report is going to the chief in the morning so he can make the press release. I just wanted you to know what happened. Thanks for calling me over that day. Who knows how long this would have been unsolved if you hadn't?"

The next day, a press conference was called. The chief explained the case had been closed, and he would go over the details during the conference. The press corps eagerly waited to see the arrest photos of the white supremacists who had beaten up the poor victim. The room was silent, however, once the reality of the claims had been spelled out. There was no mass conspiracy by the establishment. No hate crime, no white supremacist cover-up by the cops. They had all been duped.

The reporters were speechless. This was not what they expected or honestly wanted to hear. Reality is a hard teacher. The following day, a small article on one of the back pages of the local paper that the case had been resolved, and the victim admitted no such attack had occurred. Very few details were given in the article, and no one at the police department was mentioned or praised for the correct resolution of the difficult case.

CHAPTER EIGHT
DOESN'T MATTER WHERE YOU COME FROM

ONE NIGHT I WENT INTO 7-11 and found a new clerk working there. The old clerk had moved to the north end and quit to take a job closer to home. The new clerk was from New York and had a noticeable accent. Her name was Maria, and she said she was Puerto Rican, but born in New York. She was strikingly beautiful, about 5'9" with an athletic build, and long black hair. We hit it off immediately, and we started to talk when I came into the store on breaks. We shared photos of our kids and stories from our lives. She had a little girl and was a single mom working the night shift.

She became a huge draw for the store—the volume of traffic on her shifts doubled, and instantly thugs, players, and wannabe suitors from all over the city started to hang out at the store, trying to be the first to score a date with the "new girl." She felt she was more street smart, tougher, and somehow superior in her street knowledge because she was from the Big Apple.

I had heard that before—bangers would come from Los Angeles and think that they were better, smarter, and had more game. In a few short weeks, they would get a huge reality check. They were not on their home turf, and had no idea what the rules on the streets were in our city. In no time, they ended up in the emergency room, their reality checked, bodies and egos injured. No matter where you're from, you are a guest in a new city. To think your street creds followed you was ridiculous. Who you know and what you know doesn't apply in a new city. I told Maria this was not New York, and that I meant no disrespect to her street skills, but she needed to be careful. She laughed and said thanks, but she would be fine.

In no time at all, Maria had picked out who she was going to date. She had a group of wannabes to choose from, and chose a guy named Chris Blanco. Blanco was not a major player on the streets but did have a reputation for being a lowlife—a guy who abused women and had no problem walking away from friends in the middle of a fight. Basically, he was always out for himself 24/7—nothing overrode that.

They had a honeymoon dating period when Chris would actually come into the store when I was talking to her and say hi. He introduced himself, shook my hand, and always said, "Have a good day, Officer," when I left the store.

I checked him daily for warrants, looking for any reason to interrupt this façade. He laid low while he dated Maria and never got into trouble. I started to wonder if he went legit and that maybe she had turned him around. It happened occasionally—although it would be hard to believe, knowing what a dick Chris was.

I worked part-time at one of the nearby malls doing a security gig in one of the high-end clothing stores. Maria came in several times when I was at work to buy Chris clothes—not that she could afford it; she had her child to take care of and rent to pay. But Chris was a high-maintenance kind of guy and needed to be taken care of in the manner to which he was accustomed. Basically, he was the male equivalent of the trophy wife—and definitely not worth her efforts. He wanted the most expensive jackets, pants, and shoes. She bought him whatever he wanted while I watched from a distance, hoping he would try to steal something. He never did. He continued to acknowledge me with the smartass, "Have a good day, Officer," or "How are you today, Officer?" He always accentuating the "f" so it sounded like "*oFFFicer*"!

I watched and said nothing. We made eye contact, however, that made it clear where we each stood. I am sure that he thought I had something going on with Maria on a more personal level; I did not.

I just knew that Miss New York was out of her element with this shitbag, and I knew it was just a matter of time before he showed his true colors.

The shopping trips went on about three or four months, and Maria kept telling me this was the happiest she had ever been when I went into the store. Eventually, I dropped it and stopped going into the convenience store when she was working. Maybe she could handle herself after all; maybe I was wrong. Summer had kicked in, and we were in full-on emergency mode until winter storms slowed down the crime rate. I no longer had the time to wonder what was going on with Maria and her douchebag boyfriend.

Later that summer, I was feeling pretty worn down and had not seen Maria in a long time. Work was frantic in the summertime. We had to work extra shifts, and I still had the part-time jobs to keep up with. I was working at the clothing store for the third shift that week and was dead tired. I was standing in the children's clothing section at a time of day that would normally be the equivalent of 1 AM for a daywalker, watching a local "crime family" filter through the racks of kids' clothes and trying at least to slow down the rate at which they filled up their hidden bags with stolen clothing. It was a thankless task. They were expert shoplifters. While I watched them, I saw a familiar face come into the store. At first I didn't recognize the face, but as she came closer and finally spoke, I recognized it was Maria.

She looked like hell. I couldn't believe the change in her appearance. She tried to fake a weak smile and said, "Hi—do you remember me?"

I said I did, and asked her what was she doing up at this hour. She worked nights, as did I, but she didn't have to be up at *this* hour to work like I did. She moped around for a few minutes and finally said, "Can I talk to you?"

"Sure—as soon as the shoplifting Addams Family leaves I can talk," I said. "Until then, I have to keep an eye out and try to catch them."

"Yeah—I've heard about them. Word on the street is that they can get you anything." Maria even admitted to buying clothes for her daughter from them. "You know who they're hooked up with, don't you?"

"Yeah, I do. We all do, but we have no proof of any real connection; until there's proof, we just watch." Maria said nothing.

Finally, she started to breakdown and cry. I took her back into a quiet corner of the area I was watching and waited for her to tell me what had happened. I hadn't seen her or talked to her for several months. I could see the direction she was headed in hanging out with Chris, and I knew that eventually I would be seeing them on a call and I would have to deal with some ugly shit.

After a few minutes she said, "I just came to say goodbye. You were right—I should have listened to you. This city is nothing like New York. The people here are so harsh and uncaring. I didn't see it because in New York people are more in your face and direct. Here, they're all so nice, but it's a front. That's what you were trying to tell me, wasn't it?"

"Yes," I said. "The culture here…it's very much like living in a Stephen King book. What you see, what people show you, is all fake—all your friends, all your family, everyone is fake. It's hard to believe until you see through the façade."

She nodded. "I see that now."

"So what happened?" I asked.

"Well, you know—things were going really good with Chris. I thought that he was being real and honest with me. One day we talked about having a threesome with another guy, and how he'd always wanted to do that. I had no problem with that in the right context. Then, one day, he showed up at my apartment with this guy he said he wanted to 'share' with me…I have to admit I really liked it. It was awesome. A couple of days later, he showed up with another guy, and after a couple bottles of wine, I had sex with them, too—but that wasn't the same. It felt…different, less emotional, and more like I was being used."

"Then Chris showed up at my apartment one night with some guy I'd never met, and he said that he wanted to watch me have sex with him. It felt wrong. Something in the way he talked to me had changed, but I thought maybe I was just being too sensitive. Chris said that he really wanted this, and that if I loved him, I would do it."

"So what did you do?"

"I did it. I had sex with this guy while Chris watched."

I said nothing and just listened. She was really wounded but nothing she told me yet was actually the cause. "So what happened after that?" I asked.

"Isn't that enough?"

I said it was, but that I could see that there was more to this; this was not enough to make her want to leave and go back to New York. She nodded. Chris had brought three guys to where she worked, and they sat and talked for a few hours while she served customers. He told her that he would see her later that night, and she thought he meant he would be coming over alone. He didn't; he showed up with the same three guys and expected her to fuck them all while he watched.

The lines and boundaries of their relationship had quickly become very gray for her. She was about to have a painful reality check.

She said his tone of voice had completely changed; he was mean and demanding, and talked down to her, treating her like a piece of shit. Her little girl was asleep in the other room when Chris showed up with the three guys, and Maria was afraid that they would get loud and abusive and rape her if she did not fuck them willingly. She did not want her little girl to see or hear the horror that this would become, so she fucked all three while Chris watched.

When they were leaving, she saw them in the hallway of the apartment building pay Chris $30 each for letting them fuck her. She said she overheard him say that he had been "building his stable of hoodrats" and that she was his number one girl. He called her a "real freak," and said that she was up for whatever he told her to do.

Maria was crushed. She had been open to his sexual curiosity and had thought they were sharing this experience; instead, it had all been a ruse to break her down and lower her boundaries, and now he was telling everyone that he was her pimp, that she fucked for money, bought him clothes, and kept him in the lifestyle he deserved.

The reality of who and what Chris was hit her hard. Even worse, she realized that he had played her for a fool since she met him. Everyone in the city now thought of her as a prostitute. The reality of that reputation would never go away. She had no choice but to leave. She was too ashamed to stay.

She was crying harder and said, "You tried to warn me, and I thought you were just being paranoid. Everyone told me that you're paranoid as hell and always on edge, so I thought you were crazy. Now I get it. You were trying to warn me and probably were the only friend I really had here. That's why I wanted to say goodbye, and thank you for caring."

On one hand I was shocked, but not really surprised. It was hard to see her so shattered. She said that her car was packed, and she was leaving now, *right now*. She gave me a hug and walked away, sobbing.

The associate who had been working in the area came up to me and said, "You are such a fucking asshole!"

"What?" I said. "What the fuck do you mean?"

"I don't have to hear what was being said to see what just happened," she said. "You've been fucking that girl and lying to her, and she just found out that you're married and have kids, so she broke it off. Jesus, you are *such* a fucking asshole! You tell everyone how important your kids are to you, but you're a male slut just like all the other cops."

I just walked away. There was nothing to say.

CHAPTER NINE

DIGGING DEEPER

THROUGHOUT MY CAREER, I MADE a point of trying to look beyond façades into the gritty reality of what went on behind the scenes in any given situation. It always interested me to know more of what was really going on than to be the cop that *thought* he knew what was going on. It made the job a lot harder in some respects and much more interesting in others. One of the niches I loved to look into were transients that frequented the rail yards and abandoned homes in the inner city. I had some dangerous encounters with them that I have detailed in my other books. Not every stop was dangerous, but everyone I met had that potential.

Transients, for the most part, chose the life they lived. Most would admit to me they preferred the freedom of living life on the fringes of society. They were able to get free food at shelters and camp out in the rail yards, or live in abandoned houses when the weather was more pleasant. When the weather turned nasty and cold, they would simply jump a train and head south or to the West Coast where the temperature was more consistent and mild.

One of the railroad cops (they have their own dedicated police force) called me one day to show me the body of a guy who had poorly timed his trek into our state. He traveled across Wyoming and jumped onto a flatbed car loaded with lumber. He had kept a dog as a companion, and they took shelter in a small nook formed by the stacked lumber. The weather was in the mid-40s when the train left, and it was just cold; however, the train hit a brutal cold front several hundred miles before its destination. The temperature plummeted to 15 degrees Fahrenheit. Add in the wind chill of a train traveling at 50-60 mph, and suddenly it was a deadly situation. Obviously, the guy didn't plan for this and had died on the flatbed car, frozen to death. The dog survived and was protecting the body. Animal control had to be contacted before the body could be removed.

This was the reality of life on the road. You lived or died based on your choices and life skills. Choose poorly, and it was over.

Another day in the rail yards, I stopped three guys just as they got off a railcar. I started to identify them, and ran each person's information for local and nationwide warrants with the National Crime Information Center (NCIC). While I waited for a response, I spoke to the one guy who had his arm wrapped in a shirt, holding it awkwardly. I asked what happened to his arm and why he was cradling it so carefully.

He said they were attacked the night before in California. Four other men had assaulted them because their group consisted of two white men and one black man traveling together. The attackers were members of a white supremacist gang that frequented the railroad yards nationwide. They targeted anyone who wasn't white (with one exception: a Native American was a member of the group, and they had accepted him into their gang). The racists attacked the men in their California camp. They were outnumbered and taken by surprise, and it did not go well for the homeless men. They eventually fought off the gang, but during the battle, two of the supremacists held his arm in the campfire and left him with a significant burn. They told him to spread the word about why his arm was burned, and that they would be looking to attack more whites who were not "pure."

I asked him to show me the arm, and he gingerly unwrapped it. It was black—burned to the point where it was impossible to tell if any skin was left as the tendons were showing through—and his hand was frozen in a clenched fist. I said, "Holy shit, dude. That has to hurt like hell." He said it did for a while, but finally it had just stopped. He asked where he could get it treated, and I directed him to the nearest medical clinic. There was no way, in my opinion, that he would be able to keep the arm. It looked really bad.

He re-wrapped it, and the dispatcher came back with two radio codes that let me know that one of the men was wanted and dangerous. I drew my Glock and separated the men while I asked the dispatcher for the last name of the wanted man. Once dispatch gave me his name, I told the other two guys to leave and ordered the fugitive to the ground, explaining that my gun was pointed at his head, and that if he wanted to survive the day, he would do exactly as I told him. I wished the burn victim good luck with his charbroiled arm and sent him on his way. Startled by the transformation in my demeanor, both men left rapidly, thanking me for my concern.

Once I secured the suspect, I checked with dispatch and asked what he was wanted for. He had a warrant issued from our state for aggravated assault on a police officer, and they were sending backup. I explained he was already in custody and to cancel backup. I walked the arrested suspect to my car and asked him about the incident. What had happened? Why was he wanted? He claimed it must be a bar fight he was in from several years ago when he lived in the area. He was very drunk at the time and didn't remember much except that he had stabbed some guy in the head with a broken bottle. I smiled at his story. He had stabbed "some guy he didn't remember" but had immediately left town and hadn't returned for six years—until today.

On the way to jail he said, "I don't fucking care, man. Just take me to jail. It doesn't matter; I'm dying anyway."

"Dying?" I said. "What do you mean?"

He replied he had contracted AIDS when he had shared a needle with another junkie. A nurse had informed him he was HIV positive when he tried to donate plasma for money. He was screwed and dead anyway. What did he have to fear in jail? I booked him and advised the correctional officers of his HIV status. I checked, and he had stabbed a guy I worked with. I left a note in his box letting him know I had arrested the guy who had stabbed him in the head.

A year passed, and I was driving along the viaduct that overlooked the rail yards. There was a guy standing under the bridge with his back-pack and bedroll. He was waiting for a train to roll past so he could jump on. I pulled around and drove up the short dirt path to where he was standing. When I got out, he immediately dropped his pack and put his hands on his head. He remembered me from our previous encounter. It was the same guy I had arrested for the aggravated assault on the police officer a year earlier.

After I checked him out and found that he now had no warrants, I asked him what had happened. He smiled and thanked me for arresting him. I thought he was being a smart ass and asked him if he had not learned anything from the last incident.

"No, I mean it—being arrested by you was the best thing that could have happened to me. I gained 20 pounds in jail. I worked out every day, and they even gave me medication for the AIDS. I have not felt this healthy in years. I wanted to thank you, but they wouldn't call you from jail. So, it's a good coincidence that you're stopping me again in the same place you arrested me a year ago. Seriously, man—thanks." He reached out his hand to shake my hand.

"Look, you're welcome, and no disrespect, but you stabbed a cop in the head. I am not shaking your hand," I said.

"Yeah, I guess you're right! Well, take care, and thanks again."

I told him to take care as well and left, unsure how to feel about this exchange. I guess I felt good that something positive came from it.

Two hours later, I was rolling through the same area, and the guy I had stopped to talk with had moved on. This time, there was another older, and more ragged man lying on a tarp under the bridge. I stopped and tried to identify him. Eventually, after a long and diffi-cult discussion, I determined that he was schizophrenic. He could not answer any question I asked, although he did understand me. I asked for identification, and he gave me his wallet while he mumbled random nonsensical words.

I pulled out his identification and ran him for warrants. He had none; however, when I checked his wallet for other identification, I saw that he had $1800 in one hundred dollar bills. That was amazing in itself. He looked and smelled like he had not bathed or washed his clothes in over a year. His hair was wild and his beard was a ragged, gnarly mess. I asked about the money—where he got it, and why it was charred along one edge. He could not answer, but pointed to the east and rambled on in gibberish.

I thought about it for a minute and then recalled the D.B. Cooper story…could this guy have found some of the money D.B. Cooper had with him when he jumped out of that plane? I had seen some remarkable things happen. I ran the serial numbers on the money, picking out six random bills. They all came back as not stolen. The money was odd for sure, but it was not the money D.B. Cooper had stolen. I released the man and sent him on his way with his cash. He waved goodbye and muttered some random thing that had nothing to do with anything as he crawled under a bridge to go back to sleep.

A week later, I was at a family dinner. My wife at the time had a large extended family, and we went to dinner with them occasionally on Sunday afternoons. One of her cousins had recently married a guy she had gone to high school with. They had dated their entire time in high school. She was a cheerleader, and he played baseball. After high school, he had gone on a mission for the church they attended, while she earned a degree in nursing. When he returned from the mission, they became engaged and were married.

I admit I did not like the girl at all, and the feeling was mutual. To describe her as a narcissistic, lying bitch would be a compliment. I did like her new husband though, and we talked often about the cases I had handled or events related to the police department that had made it into the local newspaper. He seemed like a decent person, not at all like his wife. He came up to me as I was eating, and asked if that was me he saw under the bridge, talking to a nasty, old transient. I guess he had been driving past and saw me. I told him the story about the $1800 in the old guy's wallet.

I guess he didn't understand what I was really about as a cop, because he started to tell me that he and his friends would frequently go down into the rail yards at night and "roll the old, smelly transients for fun." I asked what he meant by that and listened carefully. He said he and four or five of his friends would get into a car and drive into the railroad yards with their lights out. They would use a hand-held spotlight to hunt transients. When they found one, they would pile out, armed with baseball bats, and beat the hell out of them. He laughed out loud, telling me what fun it was to beat the shit out of these old men, and then they stole what little money they had. "Boy, do I wish we had found that old guy with the $1800. We would have been rich!"

I stared quietly back at this fuckhead, who was wearing the chosen paraphernalia of his church—crisply pressed, short-sleeve shirt, tie, slacks, and I was sure, the special underwear that proclaimed to everyone he was one of the few "saints" worthy to enter the temple and do "God's work." Having just left Sunday school where he taught classes to small kids, he was now admitting to me that he beat the fuck out of mentally ill old men and women with *baseball bats for fun*, robbing them of what little money they had.

I was having a definite landed-on-black moment. I pushed my plate away and spoke in a quiet, yet dangerous tone.

"If I ever hear of any transient being beaten up in the rail yards, I will be knocking on your fucking door, you asshole. All I have to do is hear about an incident and detectives will have your name, and the entire conversation we just had, in a sworn statement. You are as pathetic as that bitch you call a wife! Stay away from me. Don't ever talk to me or my kids again. We clear?"

His faced turned bright red. He got up and moved to another table to finish eating. I had lost my appetite and pushed my food away. I felt like there was nowhere I could go and relax or drop my guard even for a moment.

Later, while driving home, my wife asked what was wrong. She said I was unusually quiet all night. I told her about the conversation I'd had with her cousin's new husband. She said, "He must have been trying to impress you; he would never do something like that!"

I said nothing. The fact that she thought this would somehow impress me spoke volumes. It was already painfully clear to me that she did not understand or live in the world I lived in.

CHAPTER TEN
CRUSHED LIKE A GRAPE

ONE NIGHT I GOT A call to meet a woman at the police station who had been sexually assaulted. I arrived and met with the woman and took her into an interview room. I asked what had happened, and she spoke slowly at first. She said she was recently divorced and a friend of hers had introduced her to a guy. The guy was separated and not divorced, and they had hit it off pretty well. He invited her to go camping with him and a group of friends. The camping trip was supposed to be Friday night through Sunday afternoon. She paused and said, "I was so stupid. I should have known better. No one is that nice." I sighed. This was going to get really ugly. It was obvious she was upset and had been traumatized.

She felt pretty safe with him and they had been getting along very well. The first night was pretty laid back, and they sat by a fire while he played guitar and sang campfire songs. They ate hotdogs and drank beer, told stories, and laughed. She said she liked his friends and felt really comfortable with him. The women in the group were really nice, and her friend who had introduced them was there as well.

When it came time to sleep the first night, they went into his tent and slept in separate sleeping bags. He didn't pressure her sexually, although she felt she needed to apologize to him and explained she was recently divorced, and wasn't ready for a relationship yet. He was very understanding and said he had no expectations—he just wanted to spend time with her and get to know her better. They went to sleep and spent Saturday together with the group, hiking and talking.

She had brought her car to the campsite in case things didn't go well so she could leave if she need to and not depend on anyone. Smart move, I thought, as she continued.

They drove to a nearby town and bought beer together, laughing and talking all the while. On the way back, she gave him the keys and asked him to drive, while she sat next to him in the front seat. She told him over and over how comfortable she was around him, and how he seemed like a really decent guy. He was friendly and warm, and had a good job. Nothing like her ex-husband. *He* had been abusive and a drunk, and had not held a job in quite a while. The divorce was ugly, and it was a welcome change to meet such a decent guy.

Sunday morning arrived, and after breakfast he invited her to go hiking at a lookout point high above the campground. She repeated that she hadn't felt this comfortable and relaxed in a long time. They hiked far away from everyone else, and when they reached the lookout point they stopped and stared at the mountains. She began to cry again, and I could imagine what was about to occur.

He kissed her, and at first she returned his kisses. After he tried to remove her pants, she had a change of heart, and wanted to leave. All of a sudden, he transformed from the "nice guy" she had known into a real asshole.

As she described how the attack began, I got pissed off. I had heard many stories like this, and just once I wished that a woman would realize how easy it could be to destroy the asshole attacking her if she just got mad. But the women I'd dealt with never did; they were afraid and submitted, hoping it would end quickly.

He grabbed her hair and threw her down to the ground. He started to unbutton his pants and told her one way or another, she would repay him for his kindness. He pulled out his dick and said, "*Now*, you are gonna suck my cock, bitch, and it better be good." He grabbed her hair and pulled her close to his cock and said, "Open your mouth and start sucking it."

I already knew how this would end. She had been beaten down by a bad marriage, a long and horrible divorce; she had low self-esteem, and was surely in no position to fight back. He was physically stronger than her, and she was alone and vulnerable—just like he wanted. That was what predators looked for: vulnerability.

She paused and started to cry. I handed her tissues and said, "We can go on when you're ready."

"I'm afraid what you'll think of me if I tell you the rest."

I had heard this before as well. Victims of sexual assault often thought they would be looked down upon for being raped or abused. Describing in such great detail what they had to do to survive an attack was humiliating. I told her my opinion of her would not change. She had survived the attack, and that was what mattered.

It was difficult to listen to sexual assault cases. Seeing how shattered a sexual assault victim was after an attack, whether male or female, was hard to observe without becoming homicidally angry. I admit when she finished telling me what happened, I saw her in a completely different light.

She finally continued and said he began rubbing his dick on her face, grabbed a huge handful of her hair when he was hard and said, "Okay, bitch, start sucking my cock now." She felt helpless and looked around for anyone who might help her. There was no one; he had planned his attack well. They had been seen together by several witnesses, and he had overheard her telling everyone how nice he was and how she liked him. The more she thought about it, the angrier she became. She looked up at him and gave him one last chance to stop.

"Please don't do this," she said. "Let's just walk back to camp and forget this ever happened."

"Oh, we'll walk back all right, after you finish sucking my cock and swallow my cum, you bitch. Now quit stalling and do what you were made to do."

She said something inside her snapped at that point, and she started crying again. I listened, waiting for her to tell me the horrible things she must have endured at this twisted asshole's hands.

She let out a big gasp, sobbing. "Please don't think poorly of me. I am not a bad person." I said nothing and waited for her to finish.

"I don't know what happened…" After a long pause, she continued. "Then I thought, 'Okay, I guess I have to do this,' and I leaned in like I was going to start giving him a blow job, and I just started biting. I bit his cock so hard I heard crunching and popping sounds in my mouth; I bit and bit and bit. I kept biting until he screamed and pulled me away. I think I may have crushed one of his balls. I don't know. I was so angry! I definitely felt something crush like a grape that had been bitten, through."

I was stunned. She looked at me, thinking I would be mad at her for destroying this guy's genitals. I yelled out, "YES! FINALLY! Fuck, yes! That is awesome!"

She was startled by my response. "You aren't mad?" she asked. "I mean, he was really hurt. I may have bitten it off."

"Hell, no! I'm not mad. Do you know how many times I have heard horrible accounts about some guy raping and beating a woman and wondered why she didn't do exactly what you did? This is awesome." I reached across the table and said, "High five!"

We smacked hands. She smiled.

"Wow, you really are happy about this!"

"Hell, yeah, I am! The asshole got what he deserved."

I went to get a sex crime detective to hear her story. When I returned, I had her quickly retell how she had ended the attack. The detective was sullen and quiet at first. I'm sure he thought he would have to endure another horror story. But when she detailed the popping and crunching sounds she heard as she bit her attacker over and over, the detective's reaction was exactly like mine. We were both elated that she fought back. She smiled happily, surprised at our reactions.

She finished the account and said she got up and left him there unable to walk, curled up in a fetal position. He was making horrible whimpering sounds that reminded her of a dog she had once seen that was hit by a car and left dying on the street. She walked back to camp, got into her car, and started to leave. Several of the people at the camp asked her where her male friend was, but she ignored them and left.

The detective was able to get the guy's name and address, and eventually found out where he worked. When he picked him up, the suspect said the sex was consensual and that he had done nothing wrong.

The detective obtained a search warrant, and when the suspect finally had to show the damage the woman had done, we saw that what was left of his genitalia was black-and-blue, swollen, and severely damaged. It would be permanent.

He finally admitted what he did. He said it took several hours to walk back to camp, and he had to call in sick for a few days at work. After the detective took his statement and was booking him into jail, he told me that the suspect actually said, "Haven't I suffered enough?" We both got a good laugh.

The suspect plead guilty to the attack. When I saw the woman in court at his sentencing, she said she still felt like she had done something wrong and was still mildly ashamed for having attacked him so brutally. We all told her, however, that her story was one of our new favorites to share. A sexual assault victim who had fought back and won had made our day.

CHAPTER ELEVEN

LOOKING DEEPER STILL

IN SPITE OF ALL THE deception that went on daily inside the department, dealing with the calls we went on and even in our own families, there were still some people you could always count on. Dante Holbrook was one of those guys—no matter what, you knew he'd be there if you needed him.

Physically, he was one of the most imposing people I have ever met. He was average height, but wide through the shoulders and chest to almost ridiculous proportions. His arms were at least as big as my legs, and his neck was non-existent. He looked like a cross between a man and a bear. He was normally very quiet and thoughtful, and always listened more than he spoke. Mentally, he was a perfect combination of "been there, done that."

As a younger man, he somehow made it through the tough streets of Houston, Texas. He eventually left Houston behind and moved to our city. In no time, Dante had a job working in corrections for the same sheriff's department I did. But although he did escape Texas, he brought a few of his demons with him; one was alcohol, and the other the fact that he was a mean drunk. At work he was as solid as could be; off duty, however, was a totally different story. He could not get his personal life straight, no matter how he tried.

The first time I met Dante, I was working day shift for the sheriff's department. I was the south car, (one car handled the entire southern end of the unincorporated area of the county) and was told to call the jail. I phoned the on-duty sergeant in charge, and they gave me the address of one of their employees. He hadn't shown up at work when he was scheduled to be on shift, and the sergeant was concerned. This was not usual for this employee; he always arrived early and always stayed late. The sergeant gave me the name of Dante Holbrook and asked that I try to reach him at home.

I went to the residence—an apartment—and after I'd beaten on the door for nearly three minutes, Dante opened it, pissed off, and hung-over. Once he saw that I was a deputy he said, "What? What happened? Why are you here?"

The dude was huge, filling up the doorway completely, actually turning sideways to fit his wide and muscular body through the open door. I could see his wife in the background, milling around anxiously. She looked at me briefly, and I thought it looked like she had a black eye, but it was hard to tell because the inside of the apartment was so dark. I explained to Dante that he was scheduled for work that morning, and the jail supervisor had been trying to contact him for several hours. I told him to call the booking desk as soon as possible.

He thanked me and apologized, introducing himself. "I was drinking last night, and I must have forgotten to set my alarm," he told me. He said he would call work immediately. I called the jail and let them know I had reached Dante and that he would be calling.

I did not see him again until he was hired by the city as a police officer. He was an instant hit at the department. The brass loved his tough, no-nonsense approach to the job. He quickly got a reputation as a streetwise patrol officer who was head and shoulders above the rest. He picked up a lot of overtime shifts and was a favorite of the patrol sergeants. He was very successful almost immediately, but his home life was chaotic and eventually caught up with him. I never knew for sure what happened, but rumor had it that he had been involved in a domestic dispute with his wife and had been let go from the police department. This was before the infamous O.J. Simpson trial, and domestic violence laws weren't as clear-cut and well thought-out as they are today. The police department had to let him go, and all charges were eventually dropped by prosecutors.

Dante then had a pretty successful run as a restaurant owner and setup a barbecue stand a couple of blocks from the police department. The newspaper wrote a positive review of the place, and business boomed. Dante was very successful once again, using the people skills that had served him so well as a cop to keep his business viable in the central city. Several of the guys on the force stopped to talk to Dante and ordered food from his restaurant frequently.

There were rumors on the street that Dante was hooked up with a couple of drug dealers as an enforcer and had been doing their collections as a way to make ends meet. The rumors could never be substantiated, but the fact that they existed at all made me wonder. I had learned by then that the more you looked into rumors, the more you could find out if you just knew the correct person to ask—and if you had their trust. It was whispered that Dante was a brutal enforcer.

One day after I picked up a sandwich from Dante's shop, he told me that he missed being a cop every day. He said he loved the success he had as a business owner, but his life felt meaningless since he had to resign as a cop. I left his shop and went to the report writing room to finish my paperwork while I ate.

A lieutenant walked in and started making small talk, asking about the call I was working on, and how things were in patrol. He had been a cop for a long time, and for some reason we had hit it off immediately. He asked about the sandwich I was eating, commenting that it smelled great. I told him I'd just picked it up from Dante's place. He shook his head. He wished Dante were back with us, and that he was one of the best cops he'd worked with. He remarked if Dante ever did try to come back, he would have to have his personal life together because the domestic-violence laws were not like they used to be; there were no gray areas anymore. I stopped and thought about what he was saying.

"If he did want to come back, how would that happen?" I asked.

The lieutenant said Dante would need to come in and prove himself, and prove that he had turned his life around. If they agreed to take Dante back, it would be on a very limited basis, and he would be on probation. He'd heard the rumors about Dante's status as an enforcer. Even though they were just rumors, it was "a concern."

I thought about that for a few weeks and mulled it over. Finally, I decided to hit Dante's place for another sandwich and mentioned the exchange I'd had with the lieutenant. Dante had a good rapport with him as well. I said, "Hey, man—go in and talk to him. He gave me the feeling that they might take you back if you had your shit straight and would accept an extended probation."

Dante was nearly in tears. "No shit? Really? You aren't just messing with me?" I assured him I wasn't. The brass thought the world of him, and they might really give him a second shot at being a cop. I left with my sandwich, headed back to work, and didn't think much more of the conversation.

A couple of months later, I was walking through the hallway at work, and there was Dante, wearing a community service officer's uniform. He was not a sworn police officer, but he did have a foot in the door. He'd agreed to an extended probation, but he was finally back at the police department. He came up to me in the hallway and thanked me for letting him know about the lieutenant's comments. "I would never have believed that they liked me as much as you said, but they told me that they would give me another chance." I wished him good luck.

In the community service officer role, he had access to the computer databases and reports, much like a cop would, but he had no arrest power. He could only write reports on cold calls, and he only worked day shift and swing shift. I don't know how long he worked as a community service officer. I usually worked night shift and had a couple of part-time jobs as well to try to make ends meet.

I would occasionally see Dante's wife and other members of her family in one of the clothing stores where I worked security. She had been raised in what we called a crime family, meaning the entire family led a life that kept them at odds with the police. They ran scams, did burglaries, sold stolen property, and shoplifted. All of us who worked security at the store knew about the family and their reputation, and whenever we saw them in the store we watched them closely. They would get pissed off and make a scene, calling us names and yelling as they left the store, saying we were racist pigs who only harassed them because they were Hispanic.

We did give Dante's wife a little more respect than the rest of her family, we thought that she had gone straight in actually marrying a cop. It made sense to us, since several of the cops on the force had married women who had questionable backgrounds, helping them break the family tradition of crime.

One day, however, the reality of who Dante and his adopted crime family were became extremely clear. There are two realities on the street that everyone knows. First, a secret is only a secret as long as only one person knows about it. If you tell anyone your secret, it's only a matter of time before it gets told to another person, and the network of people who know your secret will grow. Second, anyone is capable of anything given the right set of circumstances. Detectives had cultivated an informant who had information about an extensive shoplifting ring operating in the area. The informant had information that one of the local crime families had been very successful in acquiring a large amount of shoplifted and stolen property, and they were rumored to have connections to a police officer.

When the warrant was served, Dante's world came crashing down around him. He had worked his way back into the police department, but he had been lying about his real agenda. There was an amazing duality in a lot of people in law enforcement, myself included. You tried to do what you thought was the right thing, but often you couldn't choose that right thing anymore than you could sprout wings and fly.

We all have our baggage coming into this job; for some, the bags are far too heavy and cumbersome to wield. A quarter of a million dollars in stolen property was recovered from his home, and he and his wife were each charged with and convicted of multiple felonies. The property included wedding dresses, athletic shoes, and several barbecue grills. Dante claimed that he had no knowledge of the thefts or the stolen property, but it was painfully clear that he was involved in the operation from the beginning. Dante and his wife both did time for their crimes, and he was disgraced as a police officer.

CHAPTER TWELVE

STEVE: THE ENFORCER

WORKING IN THE SAME AREA night after night, week after week, you really start to know the people and their problems. There was a driveway in the middle of the block on one of the busier streets in central city that led back to a little known half-street. To the unaware, the driveway looked like any other; it was, however, the only access to this incredibly busy little street from which a lot of drug dealers were doing business from run-down houses and garages. I started to patrol this short street on foot and in my car regularly after I went on a call there.

A woman had called 911 to report that three men had forced their way into her home and were looking for her boyfriend. I walked into the area from the rear of a rundown apartment complex that had frequent drug and prostitution complaints. I decided to park there—making the apartment dwellers uneasy and interfering in their drug sales—and then walked across a small field and through a hole that had been cut in the fence. The trail was well-worn from the frequent foot traffic of drug users and streetwalkers trying to stay off our radar. I walked to the house the call had originated from and contacted the woman who had called. She was obviously afraid, but now claimed the three men were friends and that she had granted them access to the home. She no longer needed my help and asked that I leave.

That was her verbal communication; her non-verbal communication told me she was terrified. I decided to run with the non-verbal communication. I entered the home and found the three men sitting in a room, talking amongst themselves like nothing was wrong. I tried to obtain identification from them, asking them to produce it slowly, one person at a time. After obtaining and documenting who two of the men were on the field interview cards we always used, I asked the third guy, who was the biggest of the three, who he was.

"What the fuck are you gonna do if I refuse to tell you who I am?" he asked me.

There's always one guy who wants to go the hard way. "What will I do? I will call more units over here, and I will get the identification out of your pocket one way or another. The law says that if a police officer has a legitimate reason to ask you for identification, you must identify yourself. Go ahead and refuse to identify yourself, and I'll have a reason to arrest you, even if you are a guest of this woman. She called me here, so I have a reason to ask. Decision is yours. What's it gonna be?"

We had a few quiet moments, staring at each other, and sizing up the other's intentions. I was starting to not like this guy. Finally, he gave me his identification, and I recorded it on the field interview card. His name was Steve Wellington. I made a point of using his name from then on and told him he had just made a mistake. I would be watching him closely, and every chance I had I would stop him, pull him over for the slightest traffic infraction. Like it or not, I was his new best friend. Steve responded with, "Big fucking deal."

I asked the woman if she would like the men to remain in her home or leave. She replied she was tired and needed to get her kids to bed—implying that she wanted them to leave but never saying it directly. I said, "There you go, gentleman. It's time to go."

The three men left, grumbling. They said her boyfriend needed to take them seriously, and he'd better pay the money he owed. After I made sure they left, I told the woman that I would be making extra patrols at her home as often as possible. I asked about Steve and why he was so cocky. She alluded to the fact that he had a reputation on the streets as a collector and an enforcer for people who had not paid their bills.

"Your boyfriend owes someone money, and Steve was sent to collect?" I asked.

She nodded, quickly and fearfully.

"Okay, good to know. I'll be looking for Steve from now on. Get the debt paid, though, because we both know that I can only do so much, okay?" She agreed, and I left.

I asked around and found out that Steve had a brutal reputation on the street as an enforcer. He had beaten and bullied a lot of people for money, and was feared on the streets as a guy who would do whatever it took to collect a debt.

He had just become my newest pet project.

After that, I started asking around about Steve on any random call that had anything to do with drugs, or when I dealt with anyone I thought might be involved with drugs. I asked how my friend Steve was and told people to tell Steve I needed to talk to him again. This was psychological warfare on my part. He had a solid reputation on the streets as a go-to guy for drug dealers wanting to get their money, but that was about to change.

One night, I saw him in the hallway of an apartment building I had entered on another call. I walked up and called him by name. "Steve! Thanks for that information last week; it helped a lot. I owe you, man." I said it to him quietly but loud enough that his partners heard it. He said, "Hey, fuck you! I don't know you!" I heard one of his friend's say, "If you don't know him, how come he knows your name?" Steve was furious, and I smiled at him as I left.

In no time at all, maybe six months at the most, his reputation as a snitch for the cops was firmly established.

The next time I saw Steve, he wasn't so cocky. He looked worn down, and was living in an abandoned house. Neighbors had called to report that a man was staying in the abandoned home, and they wanted him gone if possible. The house had no power and no heat, and it was the middle of winter. He had been a drug user himself and since I had destroyed his reputation, he had no work, and a huge drug addiction to try and keep satisfied.

When I found him in the house, he said that I had destroyed his life and that he would get me back one day. I smiled and said, "Remember that day I told you I was going to ride your ass hard and you replied, 'Big fucking deal'? I'm just getting started, douchebag. I have your name, photo, and information now. I check you for warrants every week—and guess what? I checked yesterday, and you have a warrant."

I really had checked, and he did have a warrant for intoxication. I arrested him in the house and walked him to the car. However, instead of driving him to the jail immediately, I took my time and drove him to every known drug house, or even suspected drug house, in my area. I turned on the lights inside the car so that anyone who looked could see him inside. I then pointed at the house and pretended to be having a conversation with him, nodding my head, and making notes in a note pad. Inside the car he was calling me every name he could think of and telling me that I was a dead man. I nodded, smiled, and pointed at the house, making it look like we were having a conversation and he was giving me information.

He was seat belted in the car and obviously under arrest. Anyone who was watching from any of the houses we stopped at got the idea that he was giving up information to get out of an arrest. Of course, they didn't know that I only had him on an intoxication warrant, which meant he would be out of jail in only one or two days. It all worked against him extremely well. After I was done showing him off to every drug house in my area, I took him to jail. He was livid and screaming at me that I was a dead man when he got out of jail. I smiled and told him he had one option: leave my area for good, or I would destroy him. I left the jail and then made a point of driving past each of the houses so that they could see that Steve was no longer with me.

A week later, I got a call about a man in a park who had been beaten up. Guess who? Steve had been beaten up and dumped in a park. He had tried to buy some meth and had been told no one would sell to him. The word was out that he was my snitch. Steve, being who he was, got loud and threatening, trying to bully the dealers into selling to him. Six months earlier, he might have pulled it off. But he wasn't the huge, intimidating guy he had been. He had lost a lot of weight;

the drugs and lack of food and a safe place to stay had taken their toll. Steve got his ass kicked and dumped in the park. I called medical and paramedics took him to the hospital for treatment. I wrote up the assault, and again stopped back in every drug house in my area—this time to tell people I saw there that Steve had told me that they had beaten him up, and that I would be watching them even more now. Steve was my friend, and I would not stand for him being beaten up and dumped in the park.

I did not see Steve again for a year. He left my area and stopped trying to do anything even remotely close to my area. Then, one night, I was called to a 24-hour convenience store on the north side of the city. The call was way out of my area, but my area was unusually slow that night, so I was given the call. The clerk had called to report a suspicious vehicle in the parking lot. The occupants had been sitting in the car for over a half hour, and the clerk was afraid they were planning to rob him.

I arrived and approached the car. The driver was a female who claimed that she was just trying to look in her purse for money to buy some beer. That was the excuse for the half hour spent sitting in front of the store. I never found out what was really going on or why they were there. When I looked at her male passenger, however, I saw it was Steve. I pretended that I did not know him and asked his name. He gave me a false name and date of birth, which I wrote down and ran for warrants. The false name had none, but I didn't tell him that. I asked him to get out of the car and told him that he had a warrant. He did get out, and I arrested him for the false information. I put him in my car, and pulled out the picture that I kept of him on my visor. I said, "Remember me, STEVE?" as I showed him the picture.

He looked at me and started to cry. He had probably lost about 80 or 90 pounds since I first met him; he was exhausted and had nowhere to turn. I had destroyed any trust he had with anyone in the city. He said "Okay, okay—you win. Just let me go."

No way was that going to happen. I ran his real name and found he had two warrants. Off we went again to jail. No need to parade him through the city this time; I just took him to jail and booked him. Defeated and broken, he said nothing as the booking officers took him in.

It's the little things that make this job worth doing, and that was a good day for me. Surprisingly, though, the story did not end there.

Two years later, I was in briefing just before my shift started. I was working for Sgt. Leeds and really not enjoying it. We did not get along, and to make matters worse, I had just survived a shooting. It was my first day back at work, and Leeds told me to go to the front desk because I had a visitor. He said to hurry up and get back to briefing when I was done. I was sure that my wife at the time was having divorce papers served to me at work, announcing that not only was work a war zone, now home would become a war zone as well. Reluctantly, I went.

When I arrived at the front desk, there was a huge guy waiting for me; he asked if I was Officer Fortier. I asked who he was.

"Relax, man. You don't remember me, do you?" he asked.

I said that I did not.

"Well, for about two years, you made my life hell. You followed me and harassed me and finally made me realize I had to change my life or I would die. Do you remember me now?"

I said again that I did not. I did whatever it took to clean up my area, and his story was not unique.

"It's me, Steve Wellington," he said.

I was shocked. He had gained back at least 120 pounds. He looked healthy and actually *seemed* healthy.

I said, "Damn, man! What happened to you?"

He said, "YOU did, Officer! You made me realize I had to clean myself up or die. I was at rock bottom thanks to your fucked-up mind games, but it worked. I went into rehabilitation. I made myself a promise when I was in rehab that I would come to you and admit that you changed me and probably saved my life."

I was still not sure whether or not to believe him. We were mortal enemies. He smiled and said, "I just wanted to thank you personally for riding me so hard. I am straight, off the meth, and it's because of you."

He extended his hand and asked that I shake his. I did not. I was still jittery from the shooting, and seeing Steve did not help. Although he did look healthy and much happier, there was still real animosity in his eyes as we looked at each other. I did say congratulations and told him that I hoped he could stay off the meth. He said he understood my reluctance to shake his hand; he had been a bad dude at one time, and he deserved that. He thanked me again and walked out of the police station.

Old habits die hard. I admit I checked him for warrants as I watched him walk away. This time, however, he had none. He had really straightened out.

CHAPTER THIRTEEN

CAN'T KILL SHIT: WHAT IT REALLY MEANT

WE HAD A SAYING TO explain the strange reality we saw every day: "You can't kill shit." I was a new officer and the way they explained it to me was like this: The people we dealt with that had endured countless life-threatening injuries and always pulled out, always survived, were somehow worth less than the rest of the population. They were shit, and couldn't be killed, because they were not really of any value.

Many years later, I realized this was wrong in more ways than one. The people we saw as "shit" were just as important as the rest of us. They may have had incredibly poor coping skills—actually, horrible coping skills would be more accurate. They may have been incredibly dysfunctional, horrible parents. But they were also amazingly resilient.

I realized this while watching a man, who should have died many times over, survive yet again. He wasn't a piece of shit. Although he was far from being a shining example of what humans were capable of, he had survived perilous ocean travel in a small boat, starvation, deadly winters, a near-fatal stabbing, and mistresses who were infected with HIV. Still he survived. He could not be killed because he refused to die. Sheer willpower and a strange set of coping mechanisms kept his head up and his spirits high.

I attended a training class about officer survival that talked about this mindset and addressed the refusal to give up. Officers had died from less-than-lethal wounds on many occasions, and it was a mystery how this happened. Finally, it was theorized that they expected to die if they were ever injured in the line of duty—they literally lay down to die because they were mentally programmed to do so. I decided to adopt this "can't kill shit" mindset. When I went to work, I started the shift with the idea that I would have to fight the entire night to earn the right to survive and go home in the morning. It seems to have worked; 30 years later, I'm still here.

There was a Dumpster-diving survivor who frequented my area. He had an incredibly difficult life, while I watched from the comfortable front seat of my patrol car. See if you agree with me about the "can't kill shit" saying.

Life in the inner city—any inner city—is bleak even on its best day. I was always amazed as I was patrolling the streets, watching and policing the people who lived there, seeing how they always (well, almost always) survived stabbings, drug overdoses, shootings, and car wrecks—not to mention illness and the sheer, brutal force of the elements.

The city at night was a different animal, almost unrecognizable from the city in the daytime. There were completely different crowds of people day and night, and rarely were the two worlds aware of each other. It was hard to believe until you saw the two faces that each city has—the day city and the night city, circling each other, like yin and yang, interlocked but never touching. It was really remarkable to watch. Sometimes, however, there were people who crossed over from night to day and back again, like time travelers or magicians. They dared to venture into both worlds.

There were people who were regulars in the city at night. One was a small Cuban refugee named Osbaldo Gardenas. He was about 50 years old and maybe weighed 110 pounds on his best day. He was all of five feet tall and had some very odd personal habits. He had made his way to the United States from Cuba on a small refugee boat in the mid-80s. It was a time of political upheaval in Cuba, and a lot of mentally ill people and violent criminals were set loose to travel on small boats to the United States. I always assumed that he had come to the U.S. from Cuba as a mental patient and not a criminal since he was never aggressive or caught doing any crimes. I was never able to figure out how he ended up in our city. It could not have been an easy trek from Florida to the western U.S. but for some reason he setup his life in our inner city.

Osbaldo was one of those who made the transition between day and night look effortless. His method of survival in the inner city was Dumpster-diving. He would scavenge the Dumpsters from every apartment building and every office building, and even some homes' garbage cans if he thought he could get away with it. Anything that he could recycle for money or sell or use in any way, he kept. He had a shopping cart that he claimed as his own that he had "acquired" from an IGA superstore that was the sole source of groceries in the inner city. There was a joke among the inner city people that IGA meant "I Get Assistance," since everyone who shopped there was on welfare, food stamps, or Social Security. Times were very hard in the inner city.

Osbaldo walked the streets for hours, making a regular trek every week, trying to hit the Dumpsters before the garbage men took away his hidden treasures. As you can imagine, he smelled incredibly bad, and looked every bit a Dumpster-diver. Stained clothing, pieces of rotting food, and whatever other foul things were dumped into the large containers had been ground deep into his clothing—which, for the most part, he had also found in the Dumpster. He made the most of everything he found.

Osbaldo made enough money at this "job" to afford a small place to live in the basement of one of the older apartment houses in the inner city. But to call it an apartment, or for that matter a basement, was a stretch. It consisted of an old coal cellar and the hallway from the room where the boiler had been kept. The walls were stone and mortar, and there was only rudimentary electrical wiring. There was no toilet, and no shower. There were a few lights, a door (no windows), and a filthy bed. That was his place. I found this out one night when I was called to a report of a stabbing. I was about to learn another side of Osbaldo's unusual life.

Initial reports came in that a man had been stabbed in the basement of an apartment building. The caller said the man was seriously injured and would need medical attention as soon as possible. When the call came in, I was less than a block away. I was at the apartment building and in the basement in less than a minute. I found Osbaldo bleeding heavily from a knife wound to his left thigh. He was still conscious but very afraid. I told medical the scene was secure and had them come right in to begin treating Osbaldo. I asked Osbaldo what had happened, and he said that a crazy woman had attacked him, trying to kill him for no reason.

Frankly, it never happens that some random woman picks a Dumpster-diver to take her anger out on, so I pressed him for information while medical personnel started working on the wound. Osbaldo told me he had been having sex with a woman, and her lover had attacked him. He had such a strong Cuban accent that I had him repeat what he had to be sure I heard him correctly. I was not amazed that another woman had attacked him for being with her lover; I just had a really hard time believing he could find *any* woman to have sex with him—ever. He was incredibly disgusting on his best day.

Finally, he told me the names of the women involved and said the woman who had stabbed him was named Jackie Harris. Apparently, Jackie told him on an earlier occasion that she would carve him up if she ever caught him with her girlfriend again, and he had not listened to the threat. The girlfriend was named Tami White. Osbaldo said both Harris and White had left after she stabbed him, leaving him to die. I checked the area near the "apartment" for the knife, and found it outside, still bloody, in a garbage can. I called CSI to process the scene and asked the paramedics what his condition was. It was their opinion that he was in bad shape. He had lost a tremendous amount of blood and lived in horribly, filthy conditions. They doubted he would make it to the hospital.

This changed the nature of the call drastically. If Osbaldo was telling the truth and died, this would turn into a homicide. I announced an "attempt to locate" (ATL) for Jackie and started to look for her and Tami White. Surprisingly, I found them less than a block away, walking hand in hand like nothing had happened, happy as could be, smiling and joking. I stopped and talked to them after I let the detectives assigned to the case know that I had the suspects less than a block from the address where the stabbing had happened.

Against the odds, Osbaldo survived. After he recovered from the attack, he admitted he only pursued lesbians who were in relationships. Jackie Harris also admitted to the stabbing, and said that she had told Osbaldo to leave her property, as she referred to Tami White, alone. Since he didn't listen, she tried to kill him, simple as that. She saw no reason to lie about it or try to hide because she had warned him.

More interesting to me was how White could ever look at Osbaldo as a sexual partner. I asked her why she chose *him*. He was filthy on his cleanest day, and smelled awful. Unbelievably, she replied that Osbaldo "had it going on and could be very charming in bed." Needless to say, I was stunned. The dude must have had some gifts that were less-than-obvious because this was one of several cases I would have that involved him and his attempts to bed a member of a lesbian couple. He did, however, take them much more seriously after being stabbed, and from that point on, he always carried a knife.

A couple of years passed, and I saw White on the street one day with her new female lover. She looked pregnant, so I stopped and talked to her and her new companion. After a few minutes of small talk I asked bluntly, "Are you pregnant?"

She said yes, and that she was six months pregnant—and guess who the father was?

I thought about it a moment. "No way—not Osbaldo?" I said, shocked.

She smiled a large, toothy smile, showing a couple of new gaps in her already-compromised teeth. "Yep. Osbaldo is my baby daddy, and we three are going to raise the baby as one big family."

The two women embraced and were acting pretty happy about the idea of the baby and their family. I was horrified at the life this child would have. White was rumored to be a heroin addict, and Osbaldo would be no prize as a father. I asked White about the heroin, and she said she got clean when she found out she was pregnant. She said she could just *tell* the baby would be healthy because she had been so careful. I had my doubts.

I wish I could tell you the baby was born healthy and that they somehow pulled off this tri-parenting arrangement. The baby, however, was born an addict, underweight, and went through drug withdrawal almost immediately after being born. It died a couple of weeks later. White was charged with neglect and actually served some time. Osbaldo moved on to another lesbian partner until White got out of jail. They were on-again, off-again in the following years, living together in Osbaldo's basement dungeon apartment, sharing food and a bed. White eventually contracted AIDS through her IV drug use. Somehow she managed not to infect Osbaldo, or her girlfriend. I watched her waste away quickly after she was diagnosed, and eventually she died. This was the reality of inner city life. It was harsh and brutal and full of surprises you never saw coming, like Osbaldo and his lesbian harem.

CHAPTER FOURTEEN
BLACK-POWDER SHOOTING

HEADING HOME AFTER A RARE day shift, I was just about to hit the free-way and was driving over the overpass that crossed the rail yards that bisected the city. Just after I signed off, the dispatcher came across the handheld radio announcing that shots had been fired in the rail yard; several railroad workers had heard them and called it in. I did a U-turn, told the dispatcher I was at the scene of the shooting, and took the side street that allowed access to the frontage road that the railroad workers used to get to work. As I entered the area, I immediately saw workers pointing to a larger wooded area that we called the camps.

The transients who frequented the area setup camps in the woods, attaching makeshift tents and shelters to the trees and making small campfires to cook food and keep warm. One of the rail yard workers ran over to my car and said that several transients had come running to his building and told him that a man had been shot at least twice. He didn't know if the guy was dead or alive, but pointed at a large cluster of trees where he made his camp. I asked the worker if he got any names of witnesses, and he said no; the transients had run into his office, told him of the shooting, and then left rapidly, not wanting to get more involved than they already were.

I met up with the officer who had been dispatched to the call, and we started toward the cluster of trees where the shots were heard. We were walking through shoulder-high grass and weeds, slowly searching, guns drawn in case someone was waiting to attack us. We already knew that at least one person in the area had a gun. Transients were never without a weapon of some kind; it was necessary to survive in the world they lived in.

Searching methodically, we eventually found a camp nestled in the trees. We approached at 90 degree angles so that we would not be in crossfire if we were attacked. But no attack came. Finally, we closed in on the camp and found it in disarray. The bedding was strewn over a fallen tree, and appeared to be covering the body of a large man. All that was visible of his body was a lower left leg and his right hand, which was bloody. I called out to the body under the bedding and kicked his foot but got no response. I assumed he was dead, but years of working the streets had taught me never to assume anything. I told the other officer that I was going to pull off the bedding and to be ready for anything.

We both still had our guns drawn, and we aimed at him as I quickly removed the open bedroll. We both jumped back when the guy cried out as I removed the bedding. He was a huge man—6'7" at least, and well over 300 pounds. He yelled at us to leave him alone, and then cried out for help. When he saw that we were cops, he said, "Thank God you're here."

One of his hands was pinned under his body, and I told him to slowly pull it out and keep it in plain sight.

He replied, "I'm going to have a hard time doing that, Officer. I can't move at all."

I saw he was lying across a large log, and his left arm was pinned under his torso. I holstered my gun and asked what happened.

He said his name was Marcus McConnell, and he had been at his camp last night cooking some food when another transient entered the camp. He offered the guy some food, they ate, and shared a couple of beers. After they ate, they sat for a while watching the fire, and then the guy pulled out a gun and tried to rob him. McConnell was twice his size, so he fought back. McConnell said the guy shot him in the back, which paralyzed him, and he had fallen across the tree. Unable to move, he couldn't defend himself or stop the robbery. The robber rifled through his few possessions and took what he wanted, laughing at his now-paralyzed victim. Marcus said the robber literally pissed on him and left him to die. That was last night.

The scene did not make sense in terms of how McConnell described the robbery. He'd been covered with a bedroll when we arrived. Also, he had not responded when I kicked his foot and called out to him. I asked how he had covered himself up with a blanket if he couldn't move.

He chuckled and said, "I didn't cover myself! The son of a bitch that shot me came back today to see if I had died. When he saw that I hadn't, he shot me again, covered me up with a blanket, and left me to die." McConnell said the suspect shot him in the stomach, and he couldn't do anything except watch as the guy took his time, carefully aiming at him, and smiling when he shot him. When he heard us come into the camp, he pretended to be dead. He thought the shooter was back to finish the job. He smiled. "I never thought I would ever be so damn happy to see a cop!"

It was late October, and the nights were quite cold. It was pretty amazing that McConnell had survived the shooting and then the cold night with no protection. I asked him if he knew what kind of weapon he had been shot with.

"Yeah, it was a weird old gun, like the ones they used in the old pirate movies."

I thought for a moment and said, "A flintlock?"

"Yes—but a pistol, not a rifle like Davy Crockett's."

I started to think McConnell was hallucinating after having been in the cold so long and in such bad shape.

I called for medical and advised the dispatcher of McConnell's condition. When the paramedics arrived, we guided them back into the wooded area, and brought them to him. He was in shock by that point. Paramedics removed him carefully and rushed him to the hospital. They said his bullet wound was unusual, like no wound they had ever seen. I told them what he had said about the shooter using a flintlock pistol, and they said that it was possible.

We started to search the immediate area for witnesses but found none. Everyone we stopped we treated like a suspect, expecting them to be armed. Guess what? Everyone we stopped was armed. All had weapons. We found knives, sharpened screwdrivers, hatchets, clubs, and hammers. One guy even had a homemade handgun. It was a Derringer made out of wood, had two metal barrels with nails for firing pins, and a spring that was attached to the trigger. It was quite amazing how he had formed it. It shot .22-caliber bullets. We confiscated the gun and asked if he had actually tried to shoot it. He said yes and that it worked, although it wasn't accurate; it was, however, all he had for protection.

We took down everyone's information, and within two hours we had searched the entire area and had not found the suspect. I cleared the call and finally went home three hours later. I mentioned the shooting to my suspicious wife, telling her that was the reason I was home late from work. As usual, she didn't believe me. She had no concept of the things that I took for granted as normal in my world.

A week later, however, she had a totally different opinion of the shooting. She worked as a nurse in the same hospital where Marcus McConnell had been taken, and he had actually been housed on her floor. She had been tasked with his care, and said he was the most foulmouthed and disgusting man she had ever met. I laughed hard at that.

He had been polite and grateful to me at the scene, even shedding tears when we told him that medical was on the way and to hang in there. I told her that and she replied, "Well, he's foul! I don't know how you can deal with such foul people all day. I don't understand what you get out of that job of yours!" I smiled. I actually got along with the people on the streets better than I had with her in years.

A few days later, Marcus McConnell eventually died. He could not overcome the injuries he had sustained in the shooting and never recovered any mobility. The attempted murder had now become a murder.

As the months went by, the detectives assigned to the case eventually found out who the shooter was. His name was Dave Call. They had obtained a picture of him and learned he had a black-powder pistol.

They were quite surprised by this and said that black-powder firearms were relatively easy to purchase, as the laws at the time had a loophole that allowed their purchase with no background checks. They said it was the reason Call had purchased one; he had a criminal record, and could not buy a more conventional handgun. He had frequently purchased black-powder supplies from a local gun shop and when the detectives showed the store owner the picture of Call, he immediately recognized him. The detectives issued an NCIC warrant for him and felt it was only a matter of time before he was found.

A year and a half passed, and Call was located in a city only 15 miles from the site of the shooting. He had traveled the entire West Coast under an assumed name. Since so much time had passed since the shooting, he had started to relax, and came back to the state. He said that he thought he would be safe as long as he stayed out of our city. Eventually, I was subpoenaed to court and testified about what Marcus McConnell had said at the scene. Call gave a totally different account of the incident, and the case would be an education in how different a jury can see reality.

Call said that he and McConnell had shared a meal, and then McConnell attacked him. He said the huge man expected anal sex as payment for food. When Call refused to submit, McConnell tried to rape him. He chased Call around the camp and eventually Call had to shoot him to protect himself. That was Call's defense.

After three days of hearing the evidence, the jury made a decision in a short period of time. I was sure they would find Call guilty. McConnell was fully dressed when we found him, and had been shot twice and then covered up with a blanket and left to die. Other transients had reported the second shooting, and it was clear from the scene that McConnell had been shot twice, once in the back and once in the abdomen.

It seemed like a slam-dunk case to me; however, the jury disagreed. They found Call not guilty, and he was free to go. They later said the size difference between the two men was what made the difference to them. Marcus McConnell was a living, breathing giant; Call was 5'4" and 135 pounds. They felt that Call could not have protected himself against McConnell if his claims of attempted rape were true.

I was stunned. Every day on the job was an education. Just when I thought I could predict what would happen, I was surprised yet again. I mentioned to my wife the outcome of the case, reminding her of the giant transient she had cared for in the ICU about a year-and-a-half earlier. She again went on and on about how disgusting McConnell had been, and said that she believed he was capable of anything.

CHAPTER FIFTEEN
THE PERFECT STORM

SOMETIMES EVENTS OCCURED THAT MADE you stop and wonder. A perfect sequence of random events could make you stop and stare, stop and think quietly, *Was it possible that was actually an accident?* No one made this happen through some intricately detailed, diabolical plot; it just happened. And the momentum of the sequence of events, once it was put in motion, could not be stopped. Was there no one willing to question the direction or see the inevitable outcome? I swear that at times it seemed as if the city were some evil entity that required a sacrifice, a bloodletting to allow it to return to something resembling normal. It was eerie.

We saw this every day. A person would leave for work later than usual, or perhaps earlier than normal, and on the way to work they would be killed in a freak accident. Or maybe the person stopped to get coffee or a donut at a convenience store they normally never went to just as it was being robbed, and they were shot. The randomness of life, and more often than not death, was baffling. We would try to make sense of random events that had no significance in relation to each other, but when combined in the perfect sequence, like DNA, they could create a nightmare or a miracle. You just never knew.

Some people were destined to meet. In happy circumstances, sometimes those people were soul mates who have been looking their entire lives for each other. Sometimes, in unhappy circumstances, they were barely aware of each other until they meet, and then they might not survive the meeting. You decide whether this perfect storm was meant to be, or was simply a random sequence of events that destroyed everything in its path.

James Jones was an awkward kid raised in a middle-class family. He had an unremarkable life for the most part. He actually lived less than a block from me when my children were very small. I remembered seeing him as a teen playing in the streets as I drove to work. After high school he worked a variety of jobs, and eventually ended up enlisting in the army. He served during the Iraq and Afghanistan wars but never saw combat. He did achieve some success in the military; he completed Airborne training successfully and was honorably discharged.

He returned home after his military service and again worked a variety of jobs. But nothing seemed to fit for James. He suffered from social anxiety, and although he was friendly enough and always seemed to get along with people, he had an awkwardness about him that hinted that something was different about him. You know the kind of guy, friendly, but awkward. Somehow, though, you felt when you met them that they were just different. They didn't fit in; they were outsiders.

James found comfort in researching off-the-wall conspiracy theories, and participated in various harmless chat rooms that discussed the validity or merit of the latest conspiracy theory raising its ugly head on the Internet. He did not trust the government, which in itself was not that unusual, given how information was spun by the powers that be. James, though, obsessed about such things more than most people. He was angered by what he perceived as increasing infringement by the government into his own life and the lives of others.

He was not an immediate success after leaving the military, and eventually ended up working late nights at one of the largest retailers in America as a shelf stocker. The job suited his needs and allowed him to have minimal contact with the public, which made him more at ease. He was an odd combination: on the one hand, he was a pacifist, wanted everyone to leave him alone, and saw government conspiracies around every corner; on the other hand, he was a former army veteran who volunteered for duty to serve his country pre 9-11, and entered the army as an active-duty soldier, achieving Airborne status.

James bought a home in the center of the city. It was a small, older home that, like the man, was unremarkable, but again, it suited his needs. It blended into the neighborhood, and unless you were looking for it specifically, you would pass it by, seeing nothing memorable about it. It did, however, contain a secret that James had kept from all but his closest friends and family.

To cope with his social anxiety, James tried a variety of self-medicating options, finally settling on growing his own marijuana in the basement of his home. This was not unusual; in fact, it happened a lot more frequently than you might imagine. No matter what your views on the legalization of marijuana, the reality was that for some people, it really worked, and was definitely a better option than the multiple prescription medications pushed by doctors and pharmaceutical companies.

While I was working in the city, I knew of numerous people who had their own private pot farms in their basements, garages, or greenhouses. In 30 years of law enforcement, I never arrested one violent offender that had only used pot. Never. You would be hard-pressed to find a violent crime committed by someone who only smoked pot, and used nothing else. Alcohol was a whole other story; I won't even begin to argue *that* point.

James was working at his night job, stocking shelves until the morning hours and sleeping in the day time, growing and smoking the pot he kept in his basement. He occasionally had a girlfriend, but he was unable to maintain what most people would consider a normal long-term relationship. Already in his mid-thirties, he had no children and had never been married. His sister-in-law described him as a harmless hippie who never meant anyone any ill will. Like many people, he checked out an occasional porn site on the web. He wore costumes at Halloween parties, and even dressed up for one party as a terrorist, complete with suicide vest and traditional Islamic beard and paramilitary clothing. He was described as a clown and a prankster and, in his friends' opinions, harmless.

Living in the central part of our city meant dealing with some harsh realities that James had to face. Home invasions were a real danger, and burglaries happened often. James worked at night when most people were sleeping and was at home when most people were awake and at work. Incidentally, this was also the time when most household burglaries occurred—daytime. Burglars knew that the safest time to burglarize a home was the daytime, when everyone was at work, at school, or running errands. James was aware of this as well and purchased a 9mm handgun for protection.

He was already familiar with the weapon from his military training. The army uses the M-9 version of the Beretta, and the feeling of the gun in his hand was reassuring. He would shoot the gun maybe once a month. He would go out with family members to practice shooting—later they commented that his skill was not remarkable. He was an average or below-average shot. Skillful or not, he still felt the need to have the gun for protection. Every homeowner in the city knows that there were only so many police officers to go around. When all hell breaks loose on any given night, the cops may take up to 30 minutes responding to your own version of James's personal nightmare. He feared a home invasion, and kept his gun loaded and by his bed. This wasn't being paranoid. I kept my own firearm ready and near my bedside as well. I knew from personal experience that I would have very little time to react should this nightmare occur and someone dare to enter my own home.

James continued his unremarkable life, growing pot plants in the basement, stocking shelves at night, and enjoying living life with his extended family. Everything was pretty calm. He had a girlfriend but for whatever reason, they broke up. It happened all the time. People fell out of love or just moved on. It was a painful part of life, and very much part of being an adult. In this instance, however, James's girlfriend apparently felt slighted or wronged by the breakup. My own suspicion was that "birds of a feather" applied very much to this pair; James's coping skills were less-than-adequate, and I would suspect that his girlfriend's were as well. She plotted and planned ways to get back at James for abandoning her. "Hell hath no fury" very much applied to her.

James was unaware of a man named Conrad Carr, and that the two were on a deadly collision course. The night the two men would meet, both of their lives and the lives of their families and friends would be irrevocably changed.

———————————————

I didn't know Conrad personally, but I did interview several of his close friends and co-workers. Conrad grew up in a small town about 10 miles from the neighborhood where James grew up. He was raised in an ideal, small-town America. The streets were quiet, and the crime rates were nearly non-existent.

Later in life, his family attended a local church in which they were quite active. However, his home life as a child, was quite chaotic. He mentioned to a couple of close friends that he had memories of his parents using cocaine in the home when he was a small child. He said that wild coke parties were common and that the chaos and drama were constant.

Most cops I knew came from one kind of chaos or another. It created in them a burning desire for peace and serenity, and a conflicting desire to make a difference and contribute to society. Becoming a cop allowed them to use their chaotic life experiences to try to bring calm and safety to the train wreck that was the streets of any city. I suspected this was Conrad's goal as well. He was eager to make a difference, and perhaps battle some of the demons created by his early childhood and prove to himself that he was not bound to his parents' weaknesses. Early life experience had a way of imprinting on a child's behavioral patterns. No matter how much you craved or wanted to change who you were or where you came from, you always brought a part of that past with you.

When Conrad grew up he became a cop, and in a fairly short period of time requested and was granted a transfer to the narcotics strike force. He had married a woman who was probably the single most exciting woman he had ever met. She was beautiful, hypersexual, and without boundaries. At first, this was an exciting and addictive woman to be around. She was intensely proud of her police officer husband, as well.

The excitement the lifestyle held and the status of being a cop's wife was enticing. However, as time went on and their children were born, her constant need for chaos and risky sexual trysts became destructive to their marriage and family. Conrad himself was searching desperately for peace, while at the same time craving the intense excitement of his chaotic childhood.

Conrad lived life in a robust and enthusiastic way. He worked out feverishly—some said insanely—pushing himself to the point where he was physically sick after every workout. His personal life was a strange mixture of apparently conflicting values. He went to the same church his parents had, and said he truly believed in the religion and the values it preached, but in his own life he practiced none of them. For example, he often would go to church on a Sunday, attend services, and then afterward return home to watch his favorite football team, the Dallas Cowboys, and drink until he was drunk. He also struggled in his personal relationships with women. He frantically needed to be in a committed, loving, and emotionally monogamous relationship, but at the same time had an intense desire to sleep with other women. As you can imagine, this was nearly an impossible tightrope to walk, and it eventually began to unravel.

Conrad tried desperately to hold his family together, while being immersed in the harsh reality of the streets. Once he was transferred to narcotics, however, the strain was unbearable. The long hours and impossible demands of the job took their toll on his small family. His high-maintenance wife could not tolerate the long hours of being alone. Bored and craving chaos, she started to step out on him, engaging in trysts with other men, and women. She began to pay Conrad back for what she saw as his abandonment of her for his job. It didn't have to make sense; it was simply how she saw it. He chose work over her, and he would pay dearly for that.

Conrad was devastated when he found out about his wife's infidelity. His family was everything to him, and the thought of losing his little girls was heartbreaking. Severely depressed, and forced to work long and demanding hours in the narcotics unit, he was pushed to his limits. I spoke to several of his friends. They said he was constantly worried about his children and wanted to do whatever it took to keep his family together. The pain it caused him was obvious to everyone he knew. Eventually it became clear he had to divorce his wife and fight for the welfare of his children. He filed the paperwork, petitioning the court for a divorce, and tried desperately over and over to get custody of his children.

This was the personal hell Conrad lived working in narcotics. He constantly battled his personal demons, while trying to balance the internal conflicts he felt, looking desperately for balance and peace in his life. He was an excellent, caring, and loving father who cherished, above all else, the innocence of his small children and the peace they brought him. On the other hand, he was also an exceptional cop, and was drawn to the intensity and excitement the job offered. The streets were dangerous and gritty, and he embraced that as well. The successes he enjoyed in these aspects of his life were in direct conflict with each other, driving him into a chaotic tailspin as he tried to achieve some kind of healthy equilibrium.

My personal opinion was he was an exceptional cop *because* of these conflicts. He lived his life fast and hard, making the most of every experience and situation. However, no one can maintain this chaotic lifestyle for long, and it started to take its toll. Conrad began to suffer anxiety attacks and drank more as an attempt to cope. His "perfect life" was falling apart at the seams.

The collection of errors, betrayals, and missteps started to gather momentum, setting the two men—Conrad Carr and James Jones—on a violent collision course that would permanently derail and destroy both their lives.

James's ex-girlfriend finally found an ear that was receptive to her desire to pay James back for breaking off their relationship. She dropped an anonymous message with the narcotics strike force, detailing the marijuana growing in his basement. As I said before, I knew of several homegrown operations, and let them slide under the radar where, in my opinion, they belonged. I was tutored early on that a huge part of being a good and successful cop was knowing when to let people be human and when to enforce the law. Discretion was always one of the hardest things for a new officer to learn, and also one of the most important.

Apparently the agent who received this tip disagreed, and not only checked on the small operation, but felt it warranted a request for a search warrant. The investigating agent gathered a minimal amount of intelligence—just enough to secure the search warrant, but not enough to know what the unit would encounter when they hit the house. He felt the alleged suspect posed little threat, and the request for the search warrant described the scene of the operation as "very low risk" or "unknown." A search warrant was granted, and the narcotics squad prepared to serve it. The warrant required daytime execution, with knock-and-announce-entry.

The unit—which included Conrad Carr—was briefed in their office, and then gathered up their equipment and paperwork, preparing to hit the house before the sun officially set and the daytime search warrant expired. If it was served after sunset, it would be invalid.

For some reason, it was never adequately explained why all members of the unit weren't wearing bulletproof vests, as was required by department policy. Additionally, not all agents were clearly identifiable as police officers. Usually, the protocol was to have a uniformed officer be the first one through the door. This would leave no doubt as to what was going on—a raid being conducted by police officers, as opposed to a home invasion or a burglary. The narcotics unit works undercover, and has to look the part of drug dealers and drug users on the street in order to be effective. Consequently, their appearance was not at all what the public expected when they thought of police officers.

These two errors—not leading the raid with a uniformed officer and allowing some unit members to go into the raid without bulletproof vests—were critical. The third error was the unit's supervisor. He honestly felt that bursting into a home in the central part of the city was routine and posed no threat to any of the unit's members. That was not only incredibly stupid, but also bordered on criminal negligence on the supervisor's part. They were going to enter this home to search for drugs, while mentally unprepared and dangerously unde-requipped. I have participated in the execution of such warrants, both as a K-9 officer and a patrol officer. Being first through the door on any search warrant was never routine. To think that entering another person's home as a police officer was "routine"—for the officer or the homeowner—was ridiculous.

What happened next happened rapidly.

The unit arrived and deployed at the scene; Conrad approached the door not wearing a bulletproof vest. The team lined up on the door in typical assault-team entry style.

In these scenarios, someone usually held the door after the first guy forced it open and announced "POLICE!" loudly. (The entry was supposed to be minimally intrusive, and not alarming, but in reality it was done rapidly and violently. To be on the receiving end of such an entry was terrifying.) The guy holding the door continued to do so, while the rest of the team entered rapidly, searching the entire house, and clearing and securing each room. At least that was how it was supposed to happen. In this instance, it did not.

The team entered the home with little sense of urgency, and began searching for drugs. Remember—this was perceived by them to be a low-threat or non-threat entry, purely routine.

James Jones awoke to the sound of his door being forced open. He later claimed he didn't hear the police announce themselves, which was very believable to me. He awoke from a dead sleep, as he worked nights, so the late-afternoon entry was the equivalent of a 5 a.m. entry for the rest of the daywalker population. The laws governing search warrants were written with this in mind so they would be as unintrusive as possi-ble. Another unfortunate aspect of this raid.

After James awoke, he jumped from his bed, naked, and grabbed his gun. He thought his home was being robbed. When he looked down the hallway from the bedroom to the living room, he said he saw a group of bearded and scraggly haired men in his home. Not a single clean-cut uniformed police officer was in his line of sight.

A brutal gun battle ensued. Later, the supervisors of the unit would claim that they trained often in the correct techniques for entering a home, and that James should have known immediately that they were cops. However, the reality was you can't predict what another person perceives in a life-and-death battle. I have been in several, and it was always amazing to me what my brain chose to remember versus what actually happened. Auditory exclusion was very common; so was tunnel vision and completely missing or forgetting important facts.

James said he perceived this as a fight for his home and his life; adrenaline dumped into his body at an alarming rate, and he began the fight. When the gun battle was over, James had pushed the team completely out of his home. Remember these officers were supposed to be trained in these situations; what James did should be virtually impossible. Either James was incredibly gifted in room-to-room combat tactics, or the team, as I have said, was dangerously unprepared.

During the battle, James shot five police officers, and Conrad Carr was killed. Conrad's body was removed by his fellow officers while they tried to retreat from the no-longer-routine raid. James continued to pursue them, firing on the retreating officers from his front porch. The officers scrambled for cover, crossing his front yard, to get their bulletproof vests, which were still stored in the trucks of their under-cover vehicles. James was eventually apprehended in a shed at the rear of the home and arrested. He sustained some injuries, but none were life-threatening.

Both sides in the battle skillfully manipulated the press.

The Jones family rallied around James and said the police department had been overzealous in this raid, and had used excessive, military-style tactics in executing it. From my point of view, that's ridiculous. In fact, the truth was quite the opposite. The team was simply unprepared. A rapid, professional entry most likely would have caught James unaware in his bed, and no one would have been killed or injured. Instead, the team entered in a half-assed manner, and had their asses handed to them by a single, naked gunman with only a 9mm handgun.

The Jones family also called the police department criminals and thugs for the way they treated James once he was arrested. Again, this was ridiculous. James had just killed an undercover officer and critically wounded four others. If he had been apprehended by criminals and thugs, he would not have survived the night. He did survive, with minimal injuries, and was transported to the hospital. That fact alone was testimony to the professionalism of the officers who apprehended him.

Meanwhile, claims that child pornography and bomb-making materials had been found in James's home were published in the local newspapers. Additionally, pictures of him dressed up for Halloween as a suicide bomber were released as proof of his dangerous ties to Islamic terrorist factions. The citizens of the city should be grateful for the apprehension of this dangerous criminal. The truth was greatly distorted by both sides in this incident.

Sadly, in the end, Conrad lost his life because of a poorly planned and executed raid for a mere dozen or so marijuana plants. A few months later, while sitting in his jail cell, James Jones took his own life, choosing to commit suicide rather than face any more ridiculous court battles. The perfect storm had run its course—and once again the city had its blood sacrifice.

CHAPTER SIXTEEN

IT'S NOT FOR EVERYONE

TRAINING NEW OFFICERS MADE YOU realize the job wasn't for everyone. It changed the way you saw the world—or perhaps I should say it enabled you to see the reality of what was really going on around you. There was no escape. Your job was to see and report or record what happened accurately, cut through all the bullshit, the lies, and the deceit, and get to the bottom of whatever had happened. It could be a very ugly thing to see the world as it really was, to see people as they really were, and have nowhere to hide from it. After you were a cop for a while, you forgot that not everyone saw things that way. Not everyone was cut out for the "real world."

I had just become a field training officer when I took this call. I had a new officer riding with me, and he had already been on several calls with other officers. He had been out on the road a month or more already, and got stuck with me for a night or two because his scheduled trainer had taken a few days off.

I was working in the central part of the city as usual, and a report of a fight came in from the west side of the city. We volunteered for the call to give the new guy as much experience as possible. We drove to a small apartment building on the west side that was owned by one of the city's numerous slumlords. The owner was a self-proclaimed leader of the poorer people in the city, and managed its Head Start program, which provided him with an unlimited supply of single mothers on government assistance to rent his run-down apartments.

The apartment was a small two-bedroom, and part of a triplex of apartments that had a dirt driveway and weeds for a front yard. We parked down the street and walked in. While we were walking in and listening for anything that would tell us what was going on, I told the trainee to watch himself if we had to go into the apartment. He interrupted me and said, "I'm ready for anything. I've seen a lot in the past few months. I can handle it." I smiled and said okay. He had no idea what I was referring to, and yet here he was, cocky as hell.

We arrived at the apartment and were met by a Hispanic woman at the front door. She was a bloody mess. She told us her name was Rosie Villareal, and that her live-in boyfriend had beaten her up after they had been drinking tequila. We kept our flashlights off on our approach, and we had enough backlighting to see her hands to know she had no weapons. He had repeatedly hit her with a baseball bat, and when he finished, he left the apartment after spitting on her.

She said her face hurt and felt weird. I turned on my flashlight and checked it. The flesh on her right cheek was split apart. There was a half-inch semi-circular tear where the end of the bat had ripped the flesh and muscle apart, leaving the bone beneath exposed. Her nose wasn't just broken, it was smashed and shoved aside in the opposite direction of the tear on her check. He had severely disfigured her.

The woman was in shock, barely aware of her injuries. The new guy took down her information and called for medical response. While she waited outside, we entered the apartment to make sure the boyfriend was gone. In spite of her injuries, I had learned never to trust anything anyone told me. Often, women and men would cover for the person who abused them, and then lie to us and say the abuser had left when in fact he or she had not.

I went in first, staying away from the walls and doorways. I had been in this triplex many times, and I had learned the hard way that this small apartment building was not like most of the others in the city. The floors were carpeted, and as we walked there was a distinct crunching sound under our feet. Normally, you would assume the floor was dirty and littered with food and trash, and that that was what caused the distinct crunching noise and feeling underfoot. But, as my young trainee would soon learn, it was not.

The new guy cleared the apartment like we usually did, by the numbers—hugging a wall as he entered each room and scanned it. Moments later, he was screaming and slapping at his uniform, face, and hair. He was not yelling like he was injured or hurt; he screamed like a little girl who had just seen her first spider. I smiled and said nothing as I continued searching. The new guy left the apartment swatting at his face and uniform like he had been attacked by a swarm of bees or mosquitoes, and screaming a high-pitched, terrified little girl scream. The danger of the possible suspect lurking in the apartment had vacated his mind; now, he had other priorities.

When I was sure the suspect was gone, I walked back out of the apartment, crunching my way through the kitchen and living room. It felt like walking on Rice Krispies cereal. But that's not what it was. The crunching sound was cockroaches—thousands of them. They literally covered every wall and every flat space, including the ceiling. If you got too close to the wall, they would jump on you. That's what happened to the new guy. He hugged the wall a little too closely, and the little black "Rice Krispies" launched onto him, quickly covering him. It was creepy as fuck that anyone could live in this filth, but any inner-city cop would tell you that in our line of work, you got a huge reality check into the level of filth other people accepted as no big deal in their lives. Most people do not understand that what you see as normal in terms of cleanliness and hygiene was not necessarily what everyone else saw.

I went back outside and tried to calm the new guy. I lit him up with my flashlight and helped him brush off the remaining cockroaches. He was embarrassed by his screaming while he had tried to get the crawling bugs off his face and out of his hair. I laughed and said, "Maybe next time when I try to warn you about a call we're going to, you won't be so quick to cut me off and tell me what a badass you are. Is the big, bad cop scared of a few cockroaches?" I was being an ass and enjoying it; tormenting him was fun, but only because I pretty much had the same reaction the first time I had gone to a neighboring apartment to deal with a juvenile delinquent. I had lost my mind as well at the filth and bugs launching on me as I leaned on a doorway.

The new guy had "the crawlies" for the rest of the night. He kept imagining that he felt bugs on him, no matter where we went. It really freaked him out.

Rosie Villareal was transported to the hospital by medical personnel and admitted for treatment. Her cheekbone had been crushed by the impact of the bat, and her nose was destroyed and would need to be reconstructed. She had internal injuries as well. The detectives told me her boyfriend had sent her an article a couple of days later that he had cut out of a newspaper in Reno, Nevada. He went there to gamble and won $125,000. His picture was in the local paper. He sent it to her as a final insult— proof that she was a piece of shit and that he was better off without her. I don't know if he was ever arrested for the assault. I never saw the woman again.

Our next call sent us to another house on the west side. It was on a dead-end street, and the occupant had reported a burglary. We parked down the street and walked toward the house.

The new guy turned to me and said, "Any warning about this place before we enter?"

"No. I've never been here."

I smiled as I pretended to brush off a bug that wasn't on his shoulder. He shivered and did another complete hair, face, and body check that resembled a seizure.

We arrived at the front door of the house and knocked. There was no sound after several minutes, so I knocked harder. A woman's voice called from the side of the house. "Come to the back door, please; my dogs are inside, and I don't want them to get out."

We walked to the back door and were met by a beautiful woman wearing a shimmering thong, a sheer teddy, and nothing else. She said she just got off work at a local strip club and came home to find her house had been burglarized. She paraded around nearly nude the entire time we were there. She said, "I hope you don't mind my lack of clothing, but I'm leaving as soon as you guys are done here to entertain at a private party." I followed as the new guy started to obtain her information, and when he got to the point where he needed to know what was taken, she asked us to follow her into the house. She warned us that she had four large dogs, and that they could be pretty rowdy when she first arrived home from work. The woman walked barefoot into her home, and we followed.

As soon as we walked through the back door we were overwhelmed by the smell of dog shit. If you have ever been in a kennel that houses a lot of dogs, you can start to imagine the smell—barely. It was awful; both the new guy and I started to cough and gag. She had four large hound dogs that ran, slipping and sliding, through the shit-filled house. We stopped at the back door and looked at the floor. It was covered in dog shit several inches deep in some places. The beautiful stripper waded though it barefoot, shit squishing out between her toes as she carried on our conversation like nothing was wrong.

The sight of her dressed as she was, as pretty as she was, combined with dog shit squishing between her toes was quite a reality check. I asked if she could just tell us what items were stolen because there was no way we were going to wade through all the shit on her floors. She waved a hand at me, dismissing the comment, and said, "You all must be city folks. I grew up on a pig farm. I'm used to living with animals; it doesn't bother me at all." That was obvious as she walked around looking for her cigarettes and lighter, shit dropping from between her toes and quickly replaced by the next pile she stepped into.

She said the VCR and television were taken from her bedroom, and it was weird because that was where she kept the dogs locked up when she went to work. I looked at the new guy and he looked at me. All this filth was not because the dogs had the run of the house for the entire day. The picture of what the bedroom must look and smell like entered both of our heads. She said the dogs were in her room when she arrived home, but the VCR and TV were gone. She suspected that a guy who had spent the night with her the week before had taken the items. Our minds were trying to process the idea that anyone would choose to stay in this house filled two to six inches deep with shit, just to get laid. Granted, she was beautiful, but whoever she had brought home must have had a very different threshold of what he would go through for sex than I could imagine.

We obtained the bare minimum of information that she could provide on this lucky guy and told her we would write the report and send it to detectives. No way in hell did we have the "expertise" to handle this horrible and mysterious crime. We left in a hurry and returned to the fresh air of the city streets. The new guy was speechless as we watched the woman get into her car, still sporting the thong and sheer teddy, but now wearing huge high heels, as she headed off to whatever party she was hired for as the entertainment.

"You know," he said, "I've never been to a stripper's house before, much less one that beautiful." He paused for a moment. "THAT was not what the fuck I had expected or hoped for."

I laughed, and he laughed as well, but I could see that those two reality checks into humanity had rattled his perception of the glory that would be found working as a cop.

Eventually we cleared the call and went to the next one. The new guy, however, was not done with either of these calls. The bugs still really bothered him. Later that night, he told me he had no problem "going toes" with anyone, and that getting sent on a dangerous call did not frighten him; he would gladly go into battle to protect someone if he had to. However, he had not counted on the filth in which a lot of people lived. His idea of being the hero at a crime scene did not include being covered with cockroaches, or standing in a room full of shit.

He did continue his training and lasted about a year-and-a-half in patrol. Finally, he decided that police work was not for him, and he left to become a real estate agent. When I heard that he had quit the department, I wondered if he still felt the bugs crawling on him as he worked in his new office, or if looking at the hot new secretary made him recall the night at the stripper's home and shudder.

CHAPTER SEVENTEEN

SURVIVING THE GAUNTLET

ONE DAY YOU WOKE UP and you were the old guy in the room. Some-how along the way you forgot you were getting older. Wiser? Maybe—but definitely more jaded and less jovial. I was sitting in a training class with a roomful of younger officers when it hit me: I was the old guy in the class. Bright, shiny faces were talking energetically about the cases they had handled the night before. Seeing the enthusiasm they shared was like looking through a window into the past at the cop I used to be. I did not say much as they shared war stories, laughing in some cases over barely survived the night. Others were just glad they had avoided a disgusting projectile vomit incident with a suspect spraying vomit in their friend's patrol car.

One of the older guys in the room watched me as I watched the new officers and commented that I looked pissed off. I said I wasn't pissed; I just didn't share their enthusiasm anymore. I no longer believed my worst enemy was the suspect on the streets; my reality had been a lot different. My worst enemies were in the same uniform I wore, hiding in plain sight, waiting to strike at the first sign of weakness.

The cop I was talking to worked for one of the major depart-ments in the state. He had held a few choice assignments. Things, for the most part, had gone his way. He had not yet experienced a true reality check in his career. He shook his head and said, "Man, what's happened to you to make you so jaded and bitter? We're all in the same uniform, all a brotherhood of people who care about each other; can't you see that anymore?"

I laughed out loud, long and hard. I did remember when I thought that way, and I told him so. A couple of the younger cops noticed our conversation and listened in.

"You know what?" I said. "I am gonna predict right now that half of this class will not be cops in five years. They will be gone from the career field forever because they will do something wrong, and out the door they will go. They will trust one of their fellow cops when they get into a tough spot and find out just like I have, that there is no brotherhood anymore. It's dog-eat-dog now; the culture of the streets has changed, and the culture of law enforcement has changed as well."

I heard mumbling from the younger guys who were listening. They were saying that I was fucked up and that they hoped they would not end up like me. They shook their heads with disapproval when I said that half of the class would be gone in five years. They said that it was bullshit, that they all had long careers ahead of them making a differ-ence in the cities that they worked in.

I was the odd man out for the rest of the training. The older cop talked to me daily, picking my brain about what had changed in the career field. I told him about several of the stories I have mentioned in my books. He listened in amazement at some of the twists and turns my career had taken. He said, "Wow, man—where the hell did you work? Beirut? Chicago? Compton?" I shook my head. It didn't matter where you worked; things had changed, and you had better be aware of it or you would not survive, much less thrive, in the field.

We went out into the hallway on break and another guy approached me and quietly motioned for me to join him on a balcony that over-looked a small duck pond.

"I heard what you said in there about not being able to trust your fellow cops," he said. "I wanted to tell you a story about something that is happening right now to a friend of mine. I don't know what to think about it, and I want your opinion."

"Sure," I said, "go ahead and tell me, but don't expect me to sugarcoat my opinion. Deal?"

He agreed and began his tale. Watching his body language, I could tell that whatever the story was, it had shaken him to his core. He was forced into a place that he did not like to believe existed by the facts of this incident. He took a deep breath and started talking slowly, explaining the details of what happened.

His name was Enrique and he had been a cop for 17 years, working for several different departments, bouncing from one department to another, always looking for a bigger paycheck or a promotion. He had finally ended up leaving the money and promotions for a slower-paced job in a smaller community. He said he liked the more personal touch the smaller department had with the community it served. He said about six months before, one of the guys he worked with and was close to, had broken off a relationship with a woman who was a cop at a large department nearby. They dated for four-and-a-half years, and he began to notice she wasn't "stable," so he ended the relationship. Almost immediately, his friend's life went to shit.

"So what's the friend's name?" I asked. Enrique said his name was Manuel, but he went by Mani. A week after the breakup, Mani heard a knock at his door. The woman he broke up with had accused him of coming to her apartment and attacking her. Mani felt it was all a misunderstanding. He had an alibi: there was a video that showed him in a mall parking lot on the other side of the city, getting out of his car and entering the mall. The time stamp on the video clearly showed that he was there when the alleged assault took place. That should have cleared him.

It did not. The detective assigned to the case worked at the same department as the alleged victim. He chose to deny the alibi that the video provided and arrested Mani for assault. Since Mani and the alleged victim had also lived together, this was a domestic violence crime and that immediately suspended Mani from being able to work as a police officer. In a few short days after he had ended the relationship, he was accused of a crime, arrested, and lost his job. Mani was unable to believe what was happening. He fought the charges and was able to beat them in court and was found not guilty.

He was not allowed to return to work, however. He thought the nightmare was over, but it wasn't. The prosecutor leveled charges against Mani, again convinced by the victim that he was a danger to her and needed to be brought to justice. Mani was tried again on new evidence that his former girlfriend brought against him. She claimed he had been stalking her and had choked her outside a fast-food restaurant. Again he went to court, and once again he was found not guilty. It was an unbelievable set of circumstances to any cop who hadn't been initiated into the reality of how fucked-up some cops really were.

Enrique stared at me and said, "I just don't know what to think. Mani seems like a normal, nice guy, and it's hard to believe that he could do this kind of thing. You know, we've all seen men and women who become obsessed with their partners and feel like they are property that can never leave. I can't believe that Mani is one of those people— but this girl has injuries and the detectives believe her story. I don't know what to think. I trust my friend." Enrique looked at me. "What do you think?"

"Trust your gut," I said. "I have seen betrayal after betrayal in this job, and if you think that he's not capable of doing this, then you should believe it. Now, tell me about the girl."

Enrique said she was a "blue-flamer," driven as hell, and a very capable cop. She worked the busiest shift on the department by choice and worked in the roughest part of the largest city in the area. She was tough, fit, and capable. She had a reputation for being one of the better female cops on the department.

I smiled. This told me a lot.

"What are you smiling about?" Enrique asked.

"She is tough, capable, and street smart, well-trained and able to work in one of the worst areas in the city. That doesn't strike you as odd?" I asked.

"How so—why is that odd?"

"If she is so fucking capable, why is she suddenly pulling out the victim card? How is it that a proven performer on the street can't handle an ex-boyfriend and has to claim domestic violence? Why doesn't she just put a bullet in his ass the next time he comes close to her? Believe your friend. This bitch is lying, and the detectives she is working with should be able to see that. I can see it, and I don't even know her or your friend Mani."

Enrique nodded. "I just wish I knew what to think. I have never seen anything like this. It makes me question whether or not I can trust anyone. I don't trust my friend anymore, and now I'm starting to wonder if I can trust the other cops around me. This all just feels so wrong. One way or another, a cop is lying. I have never had to deal with this before."

I chuckled. "Dude, I envy you. I really do. I would love to be that naïve again. I could tell you shit that you would never believe is true, and none of it matters. Watch your friend's case and see what happens. I would bet a paycheck he is being setup."

I paid attention to the case from that point on. It was in the news every so often. Mani was arrested several more times after accusations by the woman cop of being terrorized by him. He was accused of aggravated sexual assault and attempted rape. He woke up one night in his *new* girlfriend's home to a SWAT team making entry into the apartment. Windows were smashed, the door was breached; Mani was removed by force, several semi-automatic rifles pointed at his head as he was arrested. He was now considered a high-risk offender who had targeted a female cop. The SWAT team was making a point of defending one of their own against what they saw as a serious threat to her life. Mani was back in jail. He could not believe the accusations against him. To say that he had lost all faith in the system and everyone who worked in it was an understatement.

He continued to maintain his innocence. Eventually his alibis and the consistency of his accounts of where he had really been, who he had been with, and what he had been doing started to outweigh the accusations made by his demented ex-girlfriend. The prosecutors started to question the validity of the female cop's claims. Her story started to unravel, and fell apart. She was arrested for lying and trying to influence a public servant. Amazingly, her chief stood behind her during the investigations. She had convinced everyone that she was the victim in this case, and the chief was included in that group of seasoned veteran cops. She was kept on paid administrative leave by the department until she actually caved in and admitted she had fabricated the entire thing. Seriously—all she wanted to do was ruin Mani for leaving her. She admitted to injuring herself, fabricating evidence, and making false statements to detectives and fellow cops about what had happened. She was arrested and booked into jail. She claimed she was sorry for all that had happened and that she never meant to hurt anyone.

The public spokesperson for the police department said that no one was more disappointed in her actions than they were, and that this was an isolated incident that was not representative of the police department. I wish I could say something meaningful about any of it. But none of it surprised me.

Mani sued the department his ex-girlfriend worked for and chose to settle out of court for a six-figure sum. His trust in the system and his passion for the job were gone. The reality of the situation he had been forced to live in had hit him hard. He now saw the world as it really was—trust no one, and nothing. That was reality. Choose to ignore it if you like.

Fast forward three years. I was in another training class at a nearby resort town. I looked over the itinerary for the training and picked out the classes I wanted to attend. The second day, I entered a class and sat in the back of the room as usual, listening to the severely overweight instructor, who also happened to be a sergeant in his department, talk about the need to always be prepared for the unexpected. He said that training yourself mentally to survive was as important as training yourself physically. It was curious to me that he saw himself as prepared in any way. He was sweating just from teaching the class. Walking back and forth in the classroom, waving his arms, and engaging the students in the topic caused him to become short of breath and develop sweat circles under his arms that should have come from an hour of hard exertion at a gym, not teaching a class in an air-conditioned room full of cops.

I looked around the room and saw that he had lost all of us almost immediately. No one was buying the bullshit this guy was selling. We were prepared, mentally and physically, to a far greater extent than this sergeant ever had been or would be. Eyes rolled as my classmates suddenly took great interest in cleaning their fingernails and scanning the training documents to look for another class to escape to at the ten-minute break.

Just as *I* was about to escape, I saw a familiar face in the class. It was the older guy I'd mentioned seeing in the previous training class. He saw me, got up, and moved to my table. We shook hands and asked each other what was new. He now had about 15 years in, and had a few more years to go before he could retire.

"So how are things?" I asked.

He looked at me long and hard, saying nothing for a long time. He finally said, "Do you remember that conversation we had at the last training we had together?"

I said I did.

"At the time, I thought you were the most fucked-up cop I had ever met. I really did. I never said anything to you, but I thought you were a real prick for the things you said about watching your back, covering your ass with your fellow cops, and that half the class would be gone from the career field in five years. Seriously, you pissed me off."

I smiled. "Yeah, I know. I have that effect on people. I've been told my whole life that I'm a prick—actually, an 'arrogant prick' is what I hear most frequently."

He laughed. "Yeah, I would agree with that assessment as well!" He shook his head and said nothing for a few minutes. Then he said, "Well, you were right, asshole."

He named off a list of cops that were now gone from the field that had been in the classroom three years earlier. One had been fired for theft, two had been fired for DUIs, one had been arrested for domestic violence—the list went on and on. It was sad to hear the toll the job had taken on their lives.

"Now I get why you are the way you are," he said.

"Why is that?"

He stared long and hard at the paper he held in his hands. Finally he started to talk. He was recently involved as an investigator on the shooting review board of his department. He was called out about three months earlier to investigate a shooting in which an officer in his department had been involved. The details were very shady, and he spoke to me in a whisper, explaining that he felt what had been declared a "good shoot" by the investigative units was, in fact, not a "good shoot."

For the first time in his career, he felt he couldn't trust his fellow cops to do the right thing. He spoke out about the shooting, that it was shady at best, and more likely than not an illegal use of force. He said no one had threatened him, but it was clear that the rest of the shooting review team did not share his opinion. They were not happy with his point of view, and made it clear that he was now an outsider.

"Now I understand what you meant that day when we talked a few years ago," he said. "I don't like how this feels. I went home after a heated argument with the others on the shooting review team and thought about the things you said in that class. I thought, fuck, that old fucker was right."

I just listened and thought to myself how many times I had heard this apology in my 30 years of working as a cop. Frankly, it sucked to see the change in him. He had been hopeful and idealistic. He hadn't experienced anything negative when we met three years earlier, and to be honest, I was envious. I missed the idealism I had seen in his eyes.

"I'm just trying to hold on until retirement," he said. "I don't love this job anymore. If I had less time on the job, I'd leave, but I'm only five years from retirement."

I understood how he felt. I had already planned to leave and finally walk away from the uniform at my 30-year mark. I had not said a word to anyone, but I knew my time was short. I told him I was sorry he had to learn what I already knew. I wished him luck, and we left the class.

He sent me an email a few months later and asked if I remembered the fat sergeant who had taught the class at the resort. I said yes—he was mister "You need to be prepared like I am," while he sweated and breathed hard just from teaching the class. He said that was him. Apparently, the sergeant was just fired for soliciting sex from a woman he had arrested. He thought I might want to know. I thanked him for the information.

The fat sergeant had been the instructor in that first classroom three years earlier when I had commented that most of the young officers in attendance wouldn't make it to the five-year mark. Now he, too, was gone from the field permanently.

CHAPTER EIGHTEEN
MEETING MR. RIGHT

THERE WERE TIMES WHEN CALLS became really personal for the entire squad. I had a domestic dispute that started in my area and lasted almost a year-and-a-half.

Emily Duchesne married the man of her dreams in her late teens. They met at a party and had an intense, emotionally charged, and very sexual six-month period of dating. A few months later, she was pregnant with her first child. Her future husband, Ken Skogsdad, begged her to marry him, and said he would take care of her and the baby for the rest of their lives. As in most relationships, there was a honeymoon period. For a while, things were perfect—too perfect. Emily was never happier and described her first year of marriage as blissful for both her and the baby. Ken really seemed like the perfect husband and father. But then the marriage began to fall apart, and soon Emily was terrified of the "real" Ken.

I was dispatched to Emily's home when the relationship was at its worst. She said Ken became brutally possessive and physically abusive. He had beaten her several times before she finally filed for a protective order and sought temporary housing in a battered women's shelter for herself and her two toddlers. She was also three months pregnant and feared for the safety of her unborn child. The beatings Ken gave her were so violent and severe, she was afraid she might lose the baby, and possibly her own life.

She requested, and was granted, the strictest protective order the state could give. Ken Skogsdad could not be within 100 yards of any location she or the children were at, no matter where she was.

Usually in the case of abusive spouses—whether men or women— they refused to let go. They never honored protective orders, and stalked and tormented the abused partner, which was the case with Ken. He was forcibly removed from their home by court order. That made him furious; his personal goal was to make Emily's life hell for daring to challenge him.

He quietly broke into the home late at night and snuck into the bedroom where Emily was sleeping. He slapped her around and terrified her until she was able to escape and call 911. When I arrived at the house, Ken was gone. I investigated the call and documented the incident. There was no sign of forced entry, and Emily had no obvious injuries. Nothing was disturbed in the home, and even the kids were still asleep. It would be hard to prove in court that this incident had happened. I placed an extra patrol on the address and made a point of checking the residence as often as I could.

Over the next six months, Ken managed to sneak into the home on random nights and terrorized Emily. Eventually, the entire squad became involved in the case, as all of us were dispatched in response to Emily's frantic calls for help.

Emily decided to move in an attempt to get away from Ken and alleviate the constant fear she lived in. Ken had lost his job, and her own financial situation deteriorated as well. She had no job, and was completely dependent on court-ordered child support and food stamps. Emily lived in her new apartment approximately 10 days and finally began to feel safe—until she woke up and saw Ken sitting in a chair next to her bed. He was just watching her sleep. He enjoyed the terror his presence alone caused, and almost never left any sign that he was in the apartment, or how he managed to enter unnoticed through locked doors.

We were all aware of the situation by this point. We setup perimeters and searched house to house whenever she called. We brought in

K-9 units and literally went yard to yard looking for Ken. He always escaped, and eventually the shift supervisor began to doubt the validity of her claims because Ken had managed to stalk her for so long while also successfully avoiding us.

There were other cases where we received calls that were fabricated purely to draw attention to the victim. Some people took advantage of the fact that we had to respond, and they made the most of the legal system, expecting us to do everything possible to solve their problems. Their need for attention wasted a lot of our time and made us suspicious of calls like this that never produced any physical evidence to support the victim's claims.

Emily moved two more times, trying to avoid Ken and the constant harassment and terror she lived daily. Nothing worked. He continued to follow her and found a way into each new place—never leaving a sign he was there. I admit that after a year-and-a-half of him avoiding capture, I was skeptical he had actually stalked Emily. No one had been this successful in evading capture. Several times I was less than a block away when the call came in, and was out of the car and at her newest apartment in less than a minute. It didn't matter; Ken was always gone and, invariably, no one had seen him except Emily. It seemed like a real possibility that Emily was making it up for attention.

The battered women's shelter raised hell with the police department at our inability to locate and arrest Ken. Shit started rolling downhill, and the chief put pressure on the duty lieutenant to resolve this case one way or another. The lieutenant made it clear that the next time we received a call from Emily it would be a squad response. We needed to end this situation.

One fall morning, Emily awoke to a noise in her latest apartment. The constant fear had taken its toll. She had lost a lot of weight, her hair was falling out, and she there were dark circles under her eyes. She looked like hell and was constantly on edge. Fortunately for her, this also made her hypervigilant as well. She was awake immediately, and alert. She heard a weird, muted noise and this time didn't. She called 911 quietly and said that Ken was in the apartment. Units arrived in a massive coordinated response. The entire city block was cordoned off, and K-9 units were waiting in strategic locations to search for Ken if he escaped.

We quietly approached Emily's apartment. She held the door open for us as we entered and made our way into the apartment. Ken was inside this time, hiding inside the furnace closet. Crammed into the small, tight space, he had no way to escape. Ken refused to go down without a fight. He was combative and had to be subdued aggressively. He was really foul—nothing like the man Emily had married. Addicted to methamphetamine, he looked and smelled rancid.

Ken was arrested, and the remaining units were called off. The lieutenant was notified that Ken had finally been captured and was on his way to jail. While we walked him to the primary officer's vehicle, he spit a huge, snot-filled mouthful of bloody spit into the officer's face.

We had to force him into the patrol vehicle, and he nearly escaped twice before we got him secured. He had extremely long hair that was knotted and bloody from the fight inside the apartment that happened during the arrest. The second time, after he'd opened the door on the patrol car after slipping out of the seat belt, one officer grabbed a handful of the hair and held Ken's head up just inside the car. Then we slammed the door shut. His hair was caught in the door, and he couldn't move. He was transported to the jail just like that, kicking, spitting, and fighting the entire way. That was the reality of arrest; it wasn't pretty, and often it could be downright brutal.

Sometimes karma had a way of taking its time to catch up to a person, and now Ken finally met karma full force. He was a special case in the court system and received the maximum punishment allowed by law. His charismatic personality did not serve him well in prison, and I was told that other inmates beat him on a regular basis. He ended up dying from injuries he received while being beaten up by an inmate he had pissed off.

Emily was finally able to move on with her life, and I never heard from her again. It always amazed me how one small decision or incident could derail a person's life. I wondered how each of their lives would have been different if Emily Duchesne and Ken Skogsdad had never met at that party.

CHAPTER NINETEEN

SMELL OF ASS IN THE CAR

ONE DAY I RECEIVED A call about a fight that broke out in an apartment building right in the heart of the inner city. It was centrally located and a favorite spot for the drug dealers and prostitutes who frequented the area. It had a long, narrow driveway that offered the only access to the rear parking lot, and a huge porch that allowed the first-floor occupants access to their apartments. The porch was used by nearly everyone in the building to watch the constant train wreck that was inner-city life. It was also frequently used by the dealers and streetwalkers to keep an eye out for us. As soon as anyone saw a cop, there was a universal signal that went out that everyone understood—a high-pitched whistle that warbled up and down the scale. I've heard that same whistle on a couple of older rap albums, so I assumed it must be universal on the street as a warning that Five-O was in the area.

I arrived to investigate the call and got out of my patrol car. Immediately the air was filled with the warbling sound as the whistling erupted, signaling to everyone who could hear that cops were in the area. I climbed the stairway to the top floor of the building and listened outside the apartment where the anonymous caller had said a fight was taking place. Sure enough, there were sounds of a struggle inside. I heard punching and the sounds of furniture being knocked over. I knocked on the door and yelled, "Police! Open the door!"

No one answered, and the fighting continued.

I checked the door. It wasn't locked, so I opened it and walked in. Once I was inside, I saw the apartment was virtually destroyed. Nearly all the furniture was broken. Two men, one white, one black, were locked in a battle, wrestling and punching each other repeatedly. Neither had gained any advantage over the other, as far as I could see, and to be honest, they both fought poorly. It was kind of comical to watch.

I stopped the fight and separated them. The occupant of the apartment was the white guy. He told me at first that the black guy had broken into his apartment and tried to rob him. He had repeatedly asked the black man to leave, but he wouldn't, so they got into a fight.

I asked the black guy if this were true, and he said it wasn't—but he didn't want to explain why he was in the apartment. I requested his identification and identified him as Jim Welte. I checked, and he had a warrant, so I handcuffed him and placed him in a chair while I tried to figure out what started the fight.

The white guy said his name was Mark Mooso. He had no idea who Welte was, and that he had just walked into his apartment and demanded money. Mooso refused and they fought. It was that simple.

Mooso was severely disfigured; his face and head looked like he'd had major reconstructive surgery, so I asked him what had happened. He said he was in a car crash and was ejected from the car when it rolled. The car had actually rolled over his head and crushed his face. He had major reconstructive surgery on his face to restore it to some semblance of normalcy. He must have been in really bad shape after the crash because nothing about his face looked normal. We talked about the crash and the surgery for about ten minutes, and then I asked him again about the fight.

He now said Welte claimed to be a pizza deliveryman and had forced his way into the apartment. I asked if he had ordered a pizza; he said no. I said, "You opened the door knowing you didn't order it?" He replied that he had. Welte was carrying pizza, and Mooso thought he could get it for free. An empty pizza box was on the floor along with the rest of the mess. Now I had something to work with.

There was no way anyone in the central city would open their door late at night for a pizza they did not order. Everyone was too aware to fall for such a stupid ruse. I asked Mooso how long he had lived in the apartment; he said two years. I told him I'd need a statement about what had happened and asked him to write it while I took Welte to my car. He said sure. I had him follow me to my patrol vehicle and gave him the forms after I put Welte in the car. Mooso returned to his apartment to write the statement.

While I waited, I asked Welte for his version. He said he'd met Mooso at a local convenience store, and they had started talking. Welte mentioned he needed a place to stay, and Mooso had invited him to stay at his apartment. They had shared the apartment for a couple of days and then tonight, for no reason, Mooso had attacked him. That was it; that was what had happened.

I rolled my eyes and sighed. "Look, maybe you aren't listening, but Mooso is up there lying his ass off in a statement. He claims you broke into the apartment, or at the very least forced your way in, and tried to rob him. Obviously, that's not what happened. You aren't stupid, and neither am I. You're going to jail no matter what because you have a warrant. Do you want bullshit charges of robbery added because you won't tell me what really happened?"

Welte looked at me for a long time and said nothing. Finally, he let out a big sigh and instantly the car was filled with a rancid smell. "Hey, hey—don't breathe on me, okay? You smell like ass," I said.

It hit me as soon as I said it. He *did* smell like ass. He smelled *exactly* like ass.

"Do you realize you smell just like the hookers on the street who give five-dollar blow jobs?" I asked. "Why is that, Jim?"

He looked down and said nothing. I rolled down the windows and said, "I'm waiting for the truth. Why do you smell like you just sucked some guy's cock?"

Jim looked out the window and said nothing for several minutes. "Maybe because I did."

"Finally, the truth. Keep going. Tell me what actually happened."

Jim started to cry. "You don't know what it's like to be a gay black man with no money and no job. I can't find anyone who will have sex with me." With tears rolling down his face, he said he put the word out on the streets to friends and anyone else who would listen, that he was looking for no-strings-attached sex with another man. A few days ago, he heard Mooso asking around about his offer. By communicating through mutual friends, they agreed to meet at a nearby convenience store called The Red Duck. They met and danced around the subject, hinting that each had heard that the other was looking for sex. Finally, they agreed to hook up at Mooso's apartment the following day.

Welte said he brought the pizza to try and make the "date" a little nicer. Although he wanted no-strings-attached sex, he still felt the need to make it more of a date. He was an "emotional guy" and said he needed to feel a connection with his sexual partners. He brought the pizza as a surprise for Mooso.

After they finished the pizza, they got down to business and took turns giving each other blow jobs. This evolved into them each agreeing to submit to anal sex. Welte was first to "catch," while Mooso "pitched." He said they had agreed to take turns and when Mooso finally finished, it was supposed to be Welte's turn.

Mooso, however, had changed his mind and wouldn't submit to anal sex. Welte was furious and demanded that Mooso return the sexual favor. They had shared pizza and blow jobs, and Welte had done his part. Mooso refused and the fight started. Welte was going to take it if Mooso would not give it willingly. Welte said that was when I arrived.

Welte sobbed during the entire story. He was really emotional, and now his nose was running. Disgusting rivers of snot ran down his face—combined with the rancid-ass smell—it was very memorable in a not-so-cool way.

As hard as it was to hear, Welte's story made a lot more sense than the random pizza deliveryman story that Mooso had told me. I asked another unit to stand by with Welte while I confronted Mooso. Another unit arrived and stood outside my patrol car, refusing to get inside. Welte smelled that awful.

I went up to Mooso's apartment, and he handed me his statement. I read through it. He did his best to try and make sense of the two stories he had told me before. It was obviously a lie; nothing made any sense in the context of the central city. I told him I knew he was lying, and that one of his neighbors said he was looking for a male sexual partner. The imaginary neighbor explained that he and Welte had been asking around about each other, and they had met up in his apartment to have sex. I asked if that was true. Mooso became really animated and angry but finally admitted it. He had been looking for no-strings-attached sex with another man for some time. He said he'd always been gay, but since his disfigurement from the car crash, he couldn't find a male companion. Then he started to cry as well.

"You don't understand!" he wailed. "I used to be beautiful, and I could get any man I wanted; now look at me! I look like a jigsaw puzzle that was put together wrong. I look like a fucking Picasso! No one wants me now."

"So what happened? Spill it—tell me all the details."

He told me nearly word-for-word what Welte had said. But he added when he gave Welte a blow job, he was intimidated by the size of his cock. He said it was huge, and there was no way he was going to let Welte destroy his ass with that huge thing.

"So, basically, he tried to rape you and you fought back?"

He said yes.

"Do you see how hard you've made it for me to get to the truth about what happened? Next time, be honest; it saves us both a lot of bullshit."

He apologized and said he didn't want to press charges. Then, in a panicked, frantic voice, he said, "I can't press charges; no one can know what happened."

"Why?"

He said his father agreed to pay for his apartment but had attached conditions for paying the bill. His father told him God had punished him for being gay by destroying his face and leaving him disfigured. Mooso said his father told him no one would want him now, and that was his cross to bear for his behavior. The only way his father would continue to pay for the apartment was if he agreed to swear off any gay relationship.

I was stunned. The pain he felt in admitting this was hard for him to hide. It was difficult to believe his father could be so harsh.

This call was a mess. I called for the shift sergeant to meet me at my car and asked for his opinion on what to do. Sgt. Duke was a 35-year veteran of the department; very little surprised him. Today, however, when I finished explaining what happened, he said, "No shit? Jesus, what a mess!" He told me to book Welte on the warrant and let the county attorney sort out the rest. Shaking his head, Duke said, "This is a first for me."

I took Welte to jail, and while he was being processed, the booking officers complained about his intense smell. They found several well-worn and tattered pictures of nude men in his pockets.

About a week after I arrested Mr. Welte, I was sent to another apartment building to investigate an unknown disturbance. This building had been a wealthy socialite's home in the 1920s. It must have been truly magnificent in its time. Now, however, it was quite different. What once had housed a single wealthy family and their servants in small quarters at the back of the house was now nine small apartments. A small, makeshift wandering hallway gave access to the different units. The building was now a twisted, tortured version of its former self.

Transients often slept in the cockroach-infested hallways during the winter, and the entire building smelled of piss and vomit. I walked down the hallway, listening to the various occupants as I passed. Someone was having very loud and enthusiastic sex in apartment four. I shuddered as I walked past; I really didn't need to hear the passionate exchange.

I arrived at apartment number eight, and the occupant opened the door. He had called to report he'd been attacked. He identified himself as Tom Adrignola and said he'd lived there for about nine months. Adrignola was at the store and bought groceries earlier in the evening, and came home to cook dinner. While he was cooking a hamburger, someone knocked on his door. He went to the door, asked who it was, and heard the familiar voice of his neighbor, Bill, in apartment number seven. He opened the door and invited Bill in. He said he offered to make Bill a hamburger, and Bill accepted. They made some small talk for a few minutes, and then Bill told him that he needed to borrow some money. Adrignola said he had no money, as he had spent the last of his social security check on food and had nothing left.

Adrignola said Bill became very angry and threatened to beat him up if he didn't give him some money immediately. Adrignola said Bill grabbed him, held his arms behind his back, and bent him over a chair while he grabbed the spatula Adrignola had just used to cook dinner. I listened while Adrignola detailed how Bill repeatedly sodomized him with the spatula. He described in great detail the rape, tears flowing down his face. He shuddered repeatedly as he described how horrible it was, that he felt incredibly violated, and no longer felt safe in his apartment. I checked the spatula and found that it was covered in bloody fecal matter and smelled like shit. I requested CSI and had them collect the spatula and put it into evidence. At first they were skeptical of Adrignola's claims, as I had been, but when they saw the spatula all doubts were erased.

I asked Adrignola if he knew Bill's last name; he said no. I requested a medical response and Adrignola was transported to the hospital to be treated for the rape. I tried to locate any information on "Bill" in apartment number seven. We had nothing in the databases about anyone living there. I checked with the hospital and they verified that Adrignola showed signs of anal penetration, and he had some bleeding and injuries from the attack. I could do no further investigation until Bill could be located. I wrote the case up and shipped it to detectives. This was some weird shit; it sounded unbelievable, but the evidence was there to support it.

Two days later, I was called in to see the detectives as soon as I came on shift. Sgt. Duke said they wanted to update me on the attempted rape by Welte as well as the spatula sodomy case.

"Jesus." Duke laughed. "I bet you're having some interesting night-mares after this past couple of weeks."

"Yeah—it *has* been weird as hell lately. What I wouldn't give for a straightforward stabbing or shooting with no anal rape involved."

Detectives said that Adrignola had made the whole story up. They checked with his mental health caseworker and found that he constantly made claims of being sodomized. Whenever they were investigated, he admitted he made up the incidents. The caseworker said Adrignola made the claims to get attention, but never before had a spatula been used, or had there been any actual signs of an attack.

When detectives interviewed Bill Wetland in apartment seven, he completely denied any contact with Adrignola, period. He said Adrignola was creepy as hell and was always inviting him over for dinner. He claimed he never accepted the offer and avoided Adrignola as much as possible. He was horrified that he was being interviewed as a suspect in the sexual assault of his next-door neighbor.

Detectives finally confronted Adrignola, and he eventually admit-ted that he had used the spatula on himself. He said he had no idea why he did it and was sorry. He just felt like he had to do something to break up the monotony.

"No shit?" I was astounded.

"Yes. Jesus, can your area get any weirder?"

I agreed that these were not the usual crimes for my area.

"Do you remember the anal rape case from last week?" they asked me.

I said I did. The detectives said the county attorney had decided not to file charges against Welte. Mooso would not cooperate with the investigation, so they had nothing to go on.

"In the future, if you could, please try to send us the run-of-the-mill stabbings, robberies, and shootings that we're used to in your area. We've had enough of the weird shit you've been investigating to last us for quite a while," they joked.

Later, I told Sgt. Duke what they'd said, and he laughed. "Just when you think the streets can't get any weirder they do."

CHAPTER TWENTY

BARBRA MAZOKO

ONE FALL NIGHT EARLY IN my career, the dispatcher asked if I was familiar with a frequent caller in my area. Her name was Barbra Mazoko. I said no, but I *had* heard her name mentioned in the hallways at work. She was someone who several officers dreaded having contact. They said she was incredibly crazy and unpredictable, and a call to go to her apartment always required at least a two-car response. The dispatcher told me Barbra had called and was having a dispute with her neighbor and wanted police.

They sent me and one other car on the call. When I arrived, I was a bit apprehensive. Barbra had quite a reputation for being unpredictable and dangerous. The other officer had dealt with her on more than one occasion and made no secret about the fact that he did not want to deal with her at all. He commented to watch everything she did and not to drop my guard with her. He said she was very erratic and would have wild emotional swings, laughing one minute, crying the next, and then became enraged the next.

As we walked to the door, I heard Barbra inside swearing wildly, screaming, and throwing things. I knocked.

"What the fuck do you want?" she screamed.

"Police! You called for us."

She came to the door and opened it. She looked at me and said, "Oh, fucking wonderful! A new guy. Probably still a fucking virgin, too, from the looks of it." She stared at me for a moment, a crazed, furious glare in her eyes. Then she said, "Okay, virgin boy—let's see if you can make my stupid fucking neighbor turn down his stupid fucking stereo."

She walked out of her apartment and pointed toward the staircase. "That fucker right there, tell him to turn down that goddamn music."

She screamed as loud as possible. The entire apartment complex knew for sure that Barbra was fired up and pissed off tonight. She wasn't just mad; she was enraged. She stormed back into her apartment and slammed the door. It sounded like a gunshot in the nighttime air.

As we walked up the stairway to the upstairs apartment, the other officer quietly said to me, "She's been like that every single time I've come here." He shook his head. "I'm afraid one day we'll have to arrest her, and that will be a fucking hard battle. She has that 'crazy person strength.'"

I listened to him and said nothing. We convinced the upstairs neighbor that it would definitely be in his best interest not to piss off Barbra anymore than he already had. He was a 19-year-old kid in his first apartment and was new in the central city. He had no idea what the woman in the apartment below was capable of. When he saw we were serious about her being someone not to mess with, he looked frightened. He wisely turned off the music. I went back down to talk to Barbra and told my backup he could clear the call. We were busy that night, and other officers needed his help a lot more than I did.

I intended to tell Barbra the music was off, and we were clearing the call. I knocked on the door a couple of times before she answered. This time, she was a completely different version of herself. She was in tears and sobbing. I was startled at the transformation. After I told her the music was off and she probably wouldn't have any more problems with her neighbor upstairs, she nodded and quietly closed the door. The change in her emotional state was drastic, and she obviously had no control over it.

Over the next few months I received an occasional call to the apartment complex, but never at Barbra's apartment. Then one night, she called again. She said there were people hiding in her apartment, and she wanted them removed. I responded to the call with no backup. It was too busy—calls were backed up and units were frantically trying to keep up all across the city. I said I'd check it out and advise if I needed assistance.

I arrived at Barbra's apartment and knocked. This time, she came to the door and answered politely. She asked me to come in and opened the door. Before I entered, I checked her hands and saw that she was carrying a knife hidden in the hand that was not holding the door. I told her I would only come in if she put the knife away.

She stared at me for a moment. "Well, aren't you the bossy one! Okay—I'll put the knife away if you promise to check out the apartment and make anyone you find leave." I agreed, and she put the knife away in the kitchen.

I checked the entire apartment and didn't find anyone or any signs that anyone but Barbra had been there. I told her that the people who were there must have snuck out of the apartment when she called, and that she was safe now. She asked me if I was sure they were gone. I said yes, and suggested she check it herself if she wanted.

She did. She looked everywhere, and at last she was satisfied that she was alone. I sat and talked to her for a few moments and finally asked why she really called. It was obvious she had called for some reason other than believing she had invisible visitors. I had seen her worked up before, and I knew if she really thought people were in her apartment and she wanted them to leave, she would have been enraged—even if they weren't real. She had a very low tolerance for stress.

Suddenly, she said, "Would you like to see my drawings?"

I noted the change of subject, but said, "Sure."

She smiled a huge smile and for the next 20 minutes showed me drawings she had done with a pencil on any piece of paper she could find. She was very talented. She could draw birds, trees, her neighbors' cars—pretty much anything you could imagine. She even showed me pictures of other officers who had been at her apartment on calls. She had drawn them all from memory.

When she was done, she looked at me and said, "To answer your earlier question…I just get lonely. Sometimes I need to hear another person's voice and know it's a real voice, and not the voices in my head. I need to see another person, have a conversation, and know they're real and not someone in my head."

"Are you schizophrenic?" I asked.

She said she was, and also bipolar. She said as long as she was on her medication, she was pretty much able to get through the day without incident, but her life was lonely, and she missed her son. He was grown up and out on his own. In mid-sentence, she switched to tell me she had been at a Black Panther meeting as a younger woman. Did I know who the Black Panthers were?

I said I did.

Surprised, she said, "I wasn't into all of their political ideology—I just figured it would be the best way to get some sexual attention. No one would have anything to do with me when I was younger because I was so fucking crazy, but the Black Panthers would pull a train on me and it felt amazing to get some attention."

She then tried to show me how many men she could take on at once, sitting on her couch, legs spread, an imaginary cock in each hand and her mouth open as she pretended to deep-throat another. I said nothing. She just stared back. Eventually, she got up, somewhat humiliated.

"Not much phases you, does it?"

"No, not much," I said. "Look, instead of calling dispatch when you want to talk, call this number." I wrote my cell phone number down on a piece of paper. "If I'm at a work and not busy, I'll stop by, but if you really need help, call the dispatcher, okay?"

She said nothing for a minute, tears welling up in her eyes. Then she quietly said, "Yes, thank you."

"No problem. But don't try to bullshit me with gangbanging stories about the Black Panthers. And if you're gonna tell me the story, don't demonstrate your techniques; I get the idea—no need to go for shock value, okay?"

Barbra agreed. She could still be vulgar and foul but for the most part she refrained from any more attempts to try and shock me.

Barbra called me many times on my cell phone and became more personable as time went on. Often, if I had a reserve or a ride-along, she would say all kinds of outrageous things just to get a reaction out of them. She still called dispatch and would request an officer to remove various imaginary people or animals from her apartment. The officers would go, check the apartment, find nothing, and clear the call, saying Barbra was off her medication again.

One night she called for an officer to come to her apartment and change her colostomy bag. She said she was serious—she said she needed help changing it and wanted a cop to respond. I got the call and went to the apartment. When she opened the door and saw that it was me, she smiled a huge smile.

"Slick, I didn't know they would send you! I'm so embarrassed."

"Really, Barbra? A colostomy bag?"

"Yeah—can you imagine the fucking horror that would have brought about in some new cop's mind? I had a whole wonderful routine worked up to totally freak them out. I was going to fart real loud and pull up my shirt to show them the bag. Fuck—I'll have to wait and use it some night you're not working."

"Do you really have a colostomy bag?" I asked.

"Wouldn't you like to know!"

"No, not really—just curious."

She smiled. "Brutally honest as always, aren't you, Slick?"

I shrugged. We talked for a while, and she told me again how lonely she was. She had met a guy and they had been dating for a while, but in the end he left. She said he told her that her weird, quirky bullshit was too much for him. I told her I was sorry.

"But the sex we had! Oh my God, Slick—can I tell you about it?"

I held up my hand and said, "No, no thanks. Save it for the new guy who comes over on your next colostomy bag call."

She burst out laughing. "Great idea!"

She showed me her latest drawings. I saw one was of the other graveyard shift officer assigned to my area. I asked about him and what she thought of him. She raved on and on about what an amazing guy he was, and that they frequently had lunch at her apartment. She said he would bring her a sandwich and they would talk. I wondered quietly if this was the "boyfriend" she had referred to earlier. I made a mental note to watch for anything he might do that was unusual as I patrolled the area. You never knew what was really going on, and who was involved in it. Sometimes the most outrageous claims would be made, and you would find they were in fact true.

One night, the mental health director called the police department and requested that an officer stop in at Barbra's apartment to see if she was okay. The director said Barbra called her personally and asked that someone come to her apartment to remove a mountain lion that she had adopted. Barbra told the mental health director that about a week earlier she had been dumping her garbage and had found a juvenile mountain lion at the garbage Dumpster. She coaxed it back to her apartment and had been feeding it meat and milk for the past week. She said it was a welcome companion the first couple days, but lately it was too fucking aggressive for her liking, and she wanted it gone.

The director hung up and thought about it. After a few minutes, she decided it would be a good idea to have a cop check out the apartment. You never knew what was really going on in a schizophrenic's mind, and the mountain lion could be a representation of anything. The director called and asked that a unit be sent to check on Barbra, explaining the situation and the exact claims that Barbra made.

The call was put in the log and made a low priority as was usual for calls that did not involve crimes in progress. It sat unattended for several hours. Finally, a unit was sent. He was a new officer and had no experience with Barbra and her shock tactics and lack of boundaries, or with the absolute glee she felt when she was able to catch someone off-guard.

On this call, she would be elated. The new officer was about to have his world rocked by Barbra at her best, and she had a front-row seat.

The dispatched officer went out to conduct a welfare check on Barbra. The details of the situation had been relayed to the officer. Additionally, the mental health director wanted a call back, explaining what was really going on and how mentally stable Barbra seemed to the officer. The officer said he would take the call and advise on backup; he had at least heard about Barbra—that she was a frequent caller—but he was sure that he could deal with her mental mind games.

The new guy arrived and signed out on the call. He walked up to the door and knocked loudly, announcing that he was a police officer. Barbra was pissed off; she had called for help several hours ago and did not like to be kept waiting.

"Finally you assholes show up! It's about fucking time!" she screamed as she opened the door.

The new guy was abrupt and cocky and asked what she needed. He said they both knew it wasn't possible for her to have a mountain lion in the apartment. He lectured her and said she needed to quit wasting the police department's time and resources on bullshit calls like this.

Barbra smiled, asking him to come in for a moment. She explained again how she had coaxed the mountain lion into her apartment, that it was now too aggressive, and she wanted it gone.

When the officer didn't believe her she screamed at him, "Do your fucking job—it's trapped in my bedroom! You go in there and tell me it's not in there, and I will kiss your ass."

They stared at each other for a moment. "Okay—I'll search the house for your make-believe mountain lion. And then you'll never call the police again with this stupid shit. Deal?"

Barbra rolled her eyes and waved a hand at him, dismissing him with, "Yeah, yeah—just check the room, smartass fucking rookie."

The officer opened the door and walked in brazenly, positive the most he might find was a kitten or a stuffed animal. Instead, he found exactly what Barbra said he would.

She had really coaxed a juvenile mountain lion into her apartment. It was now aggressive and wanted out of the apartment. Now that it had been confined to the bedroom for several hours, it was really pissed off. As the officer opened the door, the cat growled loudly. I imagine it took him a moment to process what he was seeing and then to realize that he needed to get the hell out of the room before the cat attacked. It was cornered and agitated. He left the room much more quickly than he had entered, and slammed the door as the cat launched itself against it, crashing into the door and growling more loudly.

The new officer had been taught a valuable lesson. Never, ever think you know what you'll find at a scene. Expect the unexpected. Let it unfold, and keep your eyes open. Trying to make reality fit into what you were comfortable with was a huge mistake. Barbra, on the other hand, clapped her hands with glee. She laughed out loud and taunted the cop, who was now shaking from the adrenaline and shock of seeing a large predator in the central city just a couple of feet away from him. "The crazy old bag lady isn't so fucking crazy after all, is she?" she said, laughing.

The new officer took a few minutes to gather himself, and then requested animal control to remove the large cat. It took dispatchers a few minutes to understand he was serious. Yes, there was a large mountain lion in Barbra's apartment, and it needed to be removed. Animal control did eventually remove the cat; afterwards, the officer called the mental health director and explained there really had been a mountain lion in the apartment. He was still shaken as he described the incident to her in great detail. His cocky attitude and arrogance was put firmly in check by the crazy Barbra Mazoko.

When I heard about the incident, I smiled to myself. I can imagine Barbra was elated to have caught someone off-guard and to have been able to use her mental illness to some benefit. She loved to play pranks, and shocking the cops really made her day. She had finally been successful this time—and she only had to tell the truth.

How the big cat made it into the central part of the city was never explained. However, residents frequently kept exotic animals in their apartments and houses. I had been in several apartments that were thick with huge boa constrictors and reptiles of all types. It surprised me that people could maintain them and not have the health department called.

Looking back, I imagined someone had the mountain lion as a pet until it became too big and aggressive for the person to handle. Rather than call animal control for the animal's removal and possibly receive a fine, they had simply opened the door and let it go free.

CHAPTER TWENTY-ONE
WOLF AMONG THE SHEEP

AS A CHILD, I HATED teachers. It always seemed as if they had two faces. There was the one they showed the world—the "I change the future one student at a time" face. They martyred themselves for the betterment of all children, wrapping themselves within a self-righteous façade. Their calling was to enrich the lives of every student who came into their classrooms. That's how they perceived themselves. Their "other face"— the reality I saw—was quite different.

Where I grew up, the Teacher of the Year in 1987 was a guy named Jerry Stephenson. When I was half-way through eighth grade, 12 years before Stephenson received this illustrious award, I had him as a science teacher. We didn't get along. Tired of my lack of respect for him as a teacher, he demanded that I address him as "sir." Being incredibly stubborn, I refused. Instead, I addressed him by his first name—"Jerry." His name barely left my lips before the future Teacher of the Year punched me in the mouth.

I had braces on my teeth, and the impact of his fist shredded my lips; blood poured out of my mouth all over my desk. The class was silent, now terrified of their alleged mentor. I never told my parents about the incident. I was too afraid they would simply add to the damage he had already done.

Years later, I ran into several women who were students at the same school; some even in that same science class. They remembered the incident when he punched me and shared their experiences with Jerry. Apparently, Jerry took them into the back of his science classroom where there was a "lab." He picked the prettiest girls from the class and offered them positions as student aides. He had them correct papers, take roll call—and when no one was watching—he slid his hand under their clothing and copped a feel of their 13-year-old breasts, asses, and vaginas. Our Teacher of the Year was a real gem of a human being. Several women told me the same story, so I don't doubt its validity. They all were too terrified at the time to report him.

When I first started working as a cop, I thought if you weren't on the street in the heat of the battle, you weren't making a difference. I looked down upon the guys who worked in schools and in the units that weren't on the street.

Much later, I became one of those guys. I was burnt out, and working in schools was a way for me to try and hang on until retirement. I was in survival mode 24/7. I couldn't shut down the hypervigilant awareness that had kept me alive during my time on the street. I was exhausted and desperately needed a break. I went into schools thinking I would be able to heal. Instead, it became an environment that somehow was even more traumatic than my previous experience.

Karma has a funny, twisted sense of humor—it wasn't a coincidence that I was assigned to the same middle school I had attended 30 years earlier. Right away, I formed a friendship with one of the student counselors. Her nickname was "Kat," because she loved cats. She was a weird combination of a Woodstock wannabe and a Ralph Nader supporter. I could never quite figure out where she stood on any subject since her ideology and philosophy about life were in a constant state of flux.

One day Kat would wear a tie-dyed T-shirt and sandals, her ratty hair down around her shoulders, looking like she had just walked out of *High Times* magazine. The next day she was dressed in a business suit and glossy pumps. Kat was an enigma. For some reason, she adopted me as her confidant. She did things for the kids on the "down low" without the school administrators' approval. She was able to obtain a lot of donations for the very poor students that ended up being spent on soap, toothbrushes, coats, gloves, and shoes. The kids loved her, and she took a lot of pride in seeing the difference she made. She had mentored a group of the less-fortunate kids, and seemed to be sincerely looking out for them.

I watched, cautiously optimistic, remembering well the lessons my childhood had taught me. We worked together to help several kids, and for a brief period, I started to trust her.

One day I came to school, and the principal called me into her office. She closed the door and told me that one of the students had disappeared from school the day before. After school let out, he simply vanished. He never came home and after his mother and stepfather checked his room, they found he had packed some items and left a note that he was going to see his "real" dad.

The principal said his biological father had been a violent and abusive parent, and there was a protective order preventing him from seeing the boy. He lived in another state and was forbidden any visitation with his son. Somehow, the boy had located the dad and arranged to meet him, or ran away to see him. The parents felt there was a strong possibility that Kat had arranged the meeting. The principal said there was no evidence to support the claim, but asked if I would check into it.

It took several weeks, working with both the authorities in my state and the state where the biological father lived, to locate the boy and have him safely removed from his father's residence. When police interviewed the boy and his father, they both said they had arranged to meet on their own. The details didn't add up. I asked the principal and the school district superintendent if they wanted me to look into it further. It might take several months, but I was confident I'd find out what happened. They agreed and asked that I do whatever I could.

Eventually, I was able to get the counselor to confess she had arranged the meeting between the boy and his father. She knew this had put the boy in danger. Quite frankly, she didn't care. It was more important to her to "feel needed" and to "do what she knew was right" than to worry about the boy's welfare. She felt she had a "calling," and in her heart it was the right thing to do, regardless if it endangered the boy. I gave this information to the principal, and the counselor was immediately fired. Kat left the building with her head held high, unashamed, her savior complex safely intact.

I thought about the danger Kat had placed the boy in to satisfy her intense desire to be needed. Maybe I wasn't wrong as a kid after all: teachers were not to be trusted.

———————————

Soon afterwards, another boy from the school disappeared. This one, however, was under very different circumstances.

The school had a separate building that was a secured unit. It was built in the middle of a grass field where we used to play football when I was a kid. The building was always locked, and these students were kept isolated from the students in the main building. They ate lunch as a group before the other children. They also were not allowed to socialize with the other kids, or attend any special functions at the school.

I asked the principal one day about it. She was reluctant at first, but eventually admitted the secured building housed children that were known sexual offenders. The law required that they receive an education, so the school district provided the secured building and isolated schedule and routine in an effort to meet the legal requirements. The knowledge that they were sexual predators was kept from everyone— they were afraid parents would pull their children out of school if they learned about the unit.

I was pissed that I wasn't told about this and expressed, quite bluntly, that it wasn't acceptable to keep me in the dark about things of this nature. I expected to be kept in the loop, and I made my point brutally clear. It was obvious the priorities of the school district didn't include letting parents know sexual predators were housed on campus.

A month or two went by, and the principal called me into her office again. She closed the door and let out a deep sigh.

"I know you won't be happy about this," she said, "but I have to let you know that one of the kids from the sexual offender program on campus has disappeared."

"Disappeared? How the fuck can he just disappear?"

She said he was dropped off at school by the group home where he lived and never made it to the secured building. She asked me to search the campus for the boy while she notified the school district officials.

"How old is he?" I asked. She said he was 14.

I searched the entire building, starting in the steam tunnels that ran underneath and ended on the roof. The kid was not on campus. Still, I was worried. He was considered a violent sexual offender, and the school was a target-rich environment for him. In my opinion, I felt it was too good for him to resist. I looked everywhere and didn't find a thing. He had just disappeared, like the principal said.

Several weeks passed and there was no sign of the kid. Then one day I was called to another meeting in the principal's office. The kid had reappeared out of nowhere the night before. He was found by a man and his wife, stumbling down the sidewalk, disoriented, and filthy. He was covered with cigarette burns and long, dark welts where he had been whipped with what he thought were electrical cords. When the juvenile probation officers interviewed him, he said he was grabbed from behind at school. A couple of men put a bag over his head, tied up his hands and his feet, and stuffed him into a van. They drove him to a building and put him in what he referred to as a "dungeon."

The boy said he was used repeatedly by many men over several weeks as a "fuck toy." His hands and feet were tied, and he was blindfolded. He was forced to perform sex acts on whoever showed up. They used a permanent marker to write various insults and statements all over his body that said he "liked to be used and abused sexually." His head was shaved, and he was kept nude. He lost count of how many men came to the room. They never let him see their faces or hear their names. He was beat up, and covered in bruises and abrasions from the ordeal. Then one day they just drove him to a parking lot and dropped him off. He stumbled around, lost and confused, until the couple found him.

The principal said he wasn't returning to school. I asked who was investigating the incident. She said no one, that his claims were too wild and unbelievable, and nobody believed him. I was skeptical, so I checked at the police department. Sure enough, the detective assigned to the case found the claims the kid made "too unbelievable to be real." The case was exceptionally closed. The detective said, "Besides, the sick fuck probably volunteered to be a 'fuck toy'—you know he's a sexual offender, right? My guess is that he loved every minute of it."

Listening, I thought to myself that the detective was admitting the events had happened. He believed it; he just didn't care enough to look into it properly.

I went back to my office in the school and sat staring out the window at the secured unit. I wondered if the people who had abducted the kid were still in the building, walking past me, smiling at the students while wrapping themselves in the façade of sacrifice for our youth, like Jerry Stephenson, the Teacher of the Year, had done so many years before.

The school seemed very dark and hostile after that, and I watched every adult carefully, looking for signs of anything wrong. The hope of healing and relaxing during this assignment was a thing of the past. I had to stay just as sharp as before and be even more aware of my surroundings. I was instrumental in getting a few teachers removed from the building over the next few years for various abusive acts against the kids. And yes, I enjoyed nailing every single one.

Fall turned to winter, the leaves fell and the snow came. I arrived at work early one Wednesday, and the principal again called me into her office. I was starting to hate these fucked-up meetings. She told me one of the sixth-grade girls had died the night before. The circumstances surrounding the death were unusual, and she thought I should know. I was expecting to hear sexual abuse by the girl's parents, or perhaps a babysitter, hoping it involved a crime that would enable me or another cop to take retaliatory action against those who had killed her.

Instead, the principal said the death didn't appear criminal; the girl had died from autoerotic asphyxiation. She had tied a rope to the wooden rod from which she hung her clothes in her closet, tied the other end around her neck, and leaned forward, limiting her oxygen intake while she masturbated. It was a well-known technique that has accidentally killed many people. The principal wanted to inform me of the circumstances of her death and said the details would not be released to the public. The cops were called in, and it was ruled an accident.

An accident; sure, that was possible. I wondered if the kid had Internet access. This was a pretty advanced fetish for a twelve-year-old to be experimenting with, and to me that was the issue—where had she learned about it? I spoke to the girl's parents, and they said there was no Internet access in the home. None. No smartphones, either. They felt the Internet was too much temptation for their children. They had no explanation how their daughter had learned of the fetish. It was sad, but there wasn't much that could be done.

Two weeks passed, and once again I was called in for another secret meeting with the principal. Guess what? Another sixth grader, a boy this time, had died in the same manner as the girl—autoerotic asphyxiation. The principal was alarmed by the incident and asked the police department to check into the cases to make sure they weren't part of a suicide pact. They were worried the incidents were related. The coincidence was too much to ignore.

The detective assigned to the case contacted me. He was the same detective who blew off the abduction of the sexual offender, so I didn't expect much. He admitted that he was just going through the motions to make this look good. Two kids had died masturbating; to him it was that simple. There was no obvious suicide pact, and neither child's family allowed access to the Internet at home. It wasn't that there was access and it was controlled; there was no access at all for either family. Then where did the kids learn about such an advanced and extreme sexual fetish? It baffled me, but the detective assigned to the case didn't care. He was one of the new breed of police officers hired by the chief. All he cared about were stats, arrests, and closing cases.

I was more concerned with the whys and hows of this case. I looked into possible connections that would have allowed the two kids to get access to the Internet. There were none outside of school. Additionally, the two kids didn't know each other and had no classes together. It was a mystery how they had both discovered this fetish and died from it within two weeks of each other. Somehow, I felt the incidents had to be related.

I sat in the school library one day and watched the kids access the Internet. The librarian monitored them off-and-on but not closely. I did notice that every kid that came in wanted to use the one computer that was positioned farthest from the librarian. If it was busy, they quietly went to another computer; when it was free, they would jump on it. Not only was it farther away from the only supervising adult, but she couldn't see what was on the screen due to how it was positioned. When they saw me, they got up and left the room.

I knew something was up. The school district made sure unlimited access to the Internet was not allowed. A program was installed that blocked access to anything pornographic, or any website which might contain harmful content. I asked the principal if there was a way the kids could circumvent the Internet filters in place. She checked with their tech guys. They said there wasn't a way past the filters that they knew of. Still, this was the only common location where two dead kids had access to the web. And the other kids' behavior in the library told me a secret was being kept from the adults. Somehow, they had broken through the firewalls on the Internet.

As a personal project, I was helping a gang member who was allowed to come to the school where I worked. He was a hardcore gangbanger and had grown up in one of the crime families in the city—he was also extremely intelligent. I decided to give him a shot at making it out of the gang if he wanted it. I went to one of his probation hearings and offered the judge the option of letting him stay with me at my home while he completed his probation. I explained that he was exceptional, and in my opinion, if any kid had the potential to make it out of a gang and do something with his life, it was this guy. I was offering a chance. The judge knew me well and had presided over most of my cases when I was in the gang unit. I had a perfect conviction rate on every case in which I had made an arrest. He thought it over and said, "Okay, Officer—let's try it."

The kid's name was Marvin, and he lived with me for three months. His grades went from a D-minus average to an A average. He was exceptionally intelligent and could have had a bright future. I asked him one night if he knew the secret to getting around the school's program that blocked access to pornography and websites that were off limits. He laughed and said every kid in school knew that. All you had to do was join a group on Google or MSN, and then for some reason, the filter wouldn't block access to the groups.

I checked the next day and, sure enough, any computer in the school that had Internet access allowed hardcore pornography to be viewed through groups that were managed on almost every search engine. Here was the common denominator for the two kids' deaths. I found several groups on autoerotic asphyxiation among every search engine's managed groups. I informed the principal, and she passed it along to the school district. The powers that be felt this circumvention was much too complex of a maneuver for middle school students to pull off. They tried to minimize the information until I told them I had learned about it from a student in the school. The loophole was closed immediately.

Marvin came to me one night after receiving his first straight A report card and said he wanted to go back to being a thug. He really appreciated what I had done, but he was a gang member for life and that was the life he wanted to live. His probation was completed, and I guess he thought he could continue living with me while he pursued a thug's life. I said that wasn't acceptable, which surprised him, and that he'd have to go back to the courts and become a ward of the state. Either he was done with gangs and could stay, or if he wanted to continue gang-banging, he would have to leave.

He chose to leave.

CHAPTER TWENTY-TWO

BROTHER FROM ANOTHER MOTHER

IT PROBABLY GOES WITHOUT SAYING that not everyone who became a cop had the same job goals. Everyone was motivated differently, and more often than not, those motivations clashed. Don Stephens and Riley Wilson were exceptional examples of how different two cops could be and yet work the same job—sometimes even the same shift and area. It was comical to watch how unlike they were, thought, and acted. They were rivals almost instantly, and played a variety of elaborate pranks on each other that eventually went way out of control.

Don Stephens was anything but a poster-boy cop. Maybe a movie cop but not a recruiting-poster cop. He was slightly built, had thick glasses, and closely resembled the deputy Barney Fife on the old cop show *Mayberry R.F.D.* Okay—maybe he was a greasier version of Barney. Don was not known for his personal hygiene. His hair was slicked down and combed to one side in a dull glob of dark grease. He was very thin. On his best day he might wear a shirt that was a size medium, and that would hang loosely on his bony frame. I would say he had about a 24-inch waist, which made it very hard to carry all the equipment we were required to carry on our duty belts.

People don't think about details like that. The reality was the smaller the cop's waist, the harder it was to fit all the crap you needed on the duty belt. Don's belt had no room among the various pouches, holsters, and cuff case. It was loaded. If he were working today, he would have to sacrifice one of the items to find room for his Taser. He was that thin.

Don was also an FTO, and I heard several hilarious accounts of him taking new recruits to his home (he lived within the city limits) for lunch. He would offer to make lunch, which most officers politely refused because his home was filthy. Every single trainee told me that while Don fixed himself a sandwich, he would plug his favorite porn tape into the VCR and turn up the volume. Instantly, the trainees were uncomfortable. "Man rules" clearly dictated what was expected of any man in these and similar situations: first, you never talked in the rest-room, ever, and second, you never watched porn with another guy. Don had issues like that; he just didn't understand guy rules. He was also really awkward in social settings.

I don't know if he was married; I think he was, but that did not slow down his constant search for new sexual partners. He saw women as objects and constantly searched for a new trophy to add to his collec-tion. Seriously. At first, I doubted he could even pick up a woman—he was so greasy and incredibly thin and unkempt. Surprisingly, though, he was remarkably successful. He worked a security gig in the city at a department store that was now bankrupt. It was called Lamonts, and he was their sole security officer. He used the job to supplement his income at the police department and to increase his stable of willing sexual partners.

To complete the picture, Don was a chain smoker. I don't mean the usual pack-a-day habit; I mean hardcore. As soon as one cigarette was burnt to the filter another would be lit. From the moment he woke up until he went to sleep, he smoked. It would be no exaggera-tion to say that he smoked three to four packs a day. Don, like most cops, thought very highly of himself and when he and Riley Wilson met, there was a mutual, unspoken agreement that each would look at the other in disgust.

Riley Wilson was the polar opposite of Don in almost every way. There were some traits they each shared, which I am sure aggravated them greatly. But first, the differences.

Riley was a giant of a man. He had played professional football, and several years later still carried the massive, muscular body of a lineman. He was softer now, in fact, hugely overweight. His duty belt would never lack for more real estate on which to place another holster, pouch, cuff case, Taser, pepper spray, cell phone, or man bag. You name it, he could carry two of each and he would still be able to see the belt underneath. He was incredibly strong. One night I was able to see an amazing example of what he was capable of while transporting a suspect he had a disagreement with from the emergency room to the jail. If you're interested, this incident can be found in *Curbchek Reload*.

As foul, filthy, and socially awkward as Don was, Riley was the polar opposite. He was always well-groomed, clean, and perfumed. His nails were always manicured, and his incredibly thick blond hair immaculate. Riley looked like how I would imagine the romance novel model Fabio would look if he were 50 pounds overweight. They had the same square jaw, broad chest, and thick, wavy hair. Riley and Don both liked to wear gold jewelry, and each proudly displayed heavy, masculine gold rings and watches.

While Don loved to smoke and did it virtually from sunup to sundown, Riley loved to eat. I mean *really* eat. Most of us had time to eat a small à-la-carte dish while on our lunch breaks at work. Riley saw that as a horrible way to enjoy a meal, and he frequently ordered two complete meals at a sitting on our 30-minute breaks. Riley never rushed anywhere for any reason and lived life at his own leisurely pace.

As I mentioned, Don loved pornography, and literally had a huge library of videos of nearly every genre that was legal. Riley found pornography to be disgusting and degrading to women. Riley was raised to cherish, honor, and respect women. In his mind, all women, regardless of who they were or what they had done were to be respected and honored simply for being women.

Riley not only honored and respected women, he found it incredibly offensive to swear around them. He frequently said, "One must always speak respectfully in the presence of a lady." It was a curious position for Riley to take, since he also had a well-established reputation as a man who would fuck anything that even resembled a female. He had absolutely no standards when it came to sexual conquests. Any and every available woman was an option. The only constant I could see in his lists of conquests was that they all had vaginas.

He ended up marrying one of the dispatchers who had been hired by the department. She was disgusting to most of us. She was sexually forward and made no secret that she was up for anything sexual with any of the cops. Somehow, Riley had asked her out on a date, and they had magically hit it off. Within a couple of months they had moved in together and were sharing an apartment; a few months after that, they were married. I sat in briefing one day while Riley spoke about how kind and gentle she was, and that he loved how she had completed him. It was hard not to gag and cough as he spoke about how she had been celibate for several years, having never found a man she could feel right about giving herself to until she met him. Riley saw himself as a Renaissance man, a gentlemen who had finally found his soul mate.

We all looked at each other quietly and said nothing while he described her long period of painfully held chastity. I knew that several of the guys in the room had personally experienced her ridiculous promiscuity. No one said anything to Riley, however. It was clear that Riley was happy in his ignorance. Surprisingly, as much as they were rivals, Don never said a single word to Riley about his wife. It was out-of-bounds, a do-not-cross-the-line sort of thing that was unspoken and understood. Secretly, I wondered if Don had already slept with her, and felt like he always had one up on Riley. I wondered if that was the real reason he never opened up that line of attack.

As I said, the two men were rivals, and polar opposites in many ways. Each found the other's personal habits annoying—Riley and his ridiculous politeness on one hand, Don and his horrible hygiene and chain smoking on the other. They exchanged verbal blows daily, each trying to one-up the other. More often than not, Riley won the battle. He was well-spoken and eloquent and easily dismantled the socially awkward Barney Fife look-alike, Don. Their battles became very heated and eventually Don grew tired of losing to the calm, cool, and photogenic Riley. One day, after an exceptionally heated battle, Don left the briefing room very agitated. He slammed open the door to the building and stormed off to his patrol car. Riley heckled him the entire way, politely rubbing Don's face in another humiliating loss in their ongoing verbal warfare.

Don drove around, simmering, and thought to himself, *I just need to up the ante. I need to catch this polite asshole off-guard and set him on his heels—but how?* A few hours later, an idea occurred to him. The next day, Don would get his final revenge.

At the time we still carried "wheel guns"—Model 586 Smith and Wesson .357 Magnums. Don got the not-so-bright idea to remove the real bullets from his gun and load it with blanks. He loaded all six chambers with blanks before showing up late for work, and he entered the building smiling. He wanted everyone in briefing to watch as he executed his supremely stupid prank.

Don entered the room feeling he would finally have his due. Riley would be humbled when this prank was over. Don sat down in his usual place and pretended to be angry. He said, "Riley, don't fuck with me today. I am in no mood for your bullshit." He was setting Riley up, knowing that there was no way Riley would not launch into a verbal assault right away. Riley started in on Don and immediately Don jumped up, simultaneously drawing his weapon from its holster. He let out a primal, guttural scream as he aimed the weapon at Riley's chest and pulled the trigger six times, firing every single blank.

Riley later said everything happened in slow motion, and by the time he realized that Don had pulled his weapon and was actually pointing it at him, every sound and object in the room had disappeared. He only saw the gun and was horrified as he watched, helpless, while Don shot him. Riley jerked with each imagined impact of the bullets that never left the barrel of the gun. Smoke filled the room, and the other officers sat stunned and speechless. They all believed that Don had just murdered Riley right in front of them.

The room was silent after Don fired the last shot. Riley frantically grabbed at his chest, gasping for air, waiting for the pain to set in and the blood to start pouring from the wounds. But nothing happened; the pain never came, the blood never flowed. Riley was terrified, and later admitted that he panicked and was sure that he had finally pushed Don too far.

Once Don saw the reaction on Riley's face and realized his stupid prank had worked, he started to laugh—a mean, maniacal, insane laugh. He said he couldn't stop laughing while he watched Riley, the aristocratic wannabe, grabbing at his chest, experiencing real panic, and being knocked off his holier-than-thou pedestal.

Don dropped the blanks out of the cylinder to show everyone in the room that he hadn't really shot Riley. It was pure dumb luck that the prank worked and that none of the other cops shot Don. He later said that had never occurred to him. Yep—Don was not real methodical when he thought this prank out.

Riley saw the blanks drop and realized that Don had pulled one over on him. He was relieved not to have been shot but realized he needed to recover his status quickly as lead dog. He got up and said, "You little fucker—I'll show you!"

Riley grabbed Don by the collar and dragged him to a nearby window. He threw it open and forced Don out of it. Riley held Don upside down, holding his bony ankle with just one hand. He shook Don up and down violently, his already incredible strength peaking from the adrenaline flowing through him.

Don had one real fear: he was terrified of heights. And he was now upside down, hanging from one ankle three-stories above the ground. Riley shook him brutally for several minutes until Don's pockets had completely emptied onto the streets below, his greasy glasses fell off, and several of the pouches on his tightly packed duty belt were emptied. Don was screaming like a little girl, begging to be brought back into the room. Riley, however, had other ideas. He held Don at arm's length, dangling him like a puppet, demanding an apology. The room behind the two men erupted in laughter. Finally, Don gave in and apologized to Riley. He had to repeat the apology over and over, before Riley was satisfied and pulled him back inside.

Once inside, Don, obviously being not too bright, started mouthing off to Riley, calling him a fucking asshole. The other cops in the room separated the two men, letting them cool off from the quid pro quo exchange of pranks. Trembling, Don walked shakily down the three flights of stairs to the street, and collected all of his belongings from outside the building. He returned to briefing and sat quietly.

Each man had earned a new respect for the other. In the space of a few minutes, they had each experienced a near-death trauma at the hands of the other. Perhaps realizing that it wasn't wise to continue this battle, they decided to call a truce.

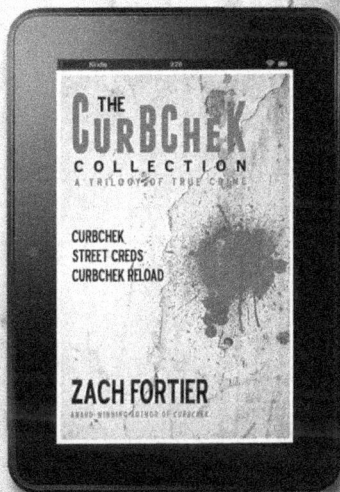

THE GOOD, THE BAD AND THE UGLY OF
LAW ENFORCEMENT ARE ALL HERE IN
ONE AWARD-WINNING COLLECTION!

THE CurBCheK
COLLECTION

FROM AWARD-WINNING AUTHOR
ZACH FORTIER

A TRILOGY OF
TRUE CRIME

CURBCHEK
STREET CREDS
CURBCHEK RELOAD

AVAILABLE IN TRADE SOFTCOVER AND EBOOK
ALL TITLES ALSO AVAILABLE SEPARATELY IN AUDIOBOOK

ZACH FORTIER WAS A POLICE officer for over 30 years specializing in K-9, SWAT, gang, domestic violence, and sex crimes as an investigator. He has written five books about his police work, including *Curb-Chek*, which won the bronze award for True Crime in the 2013 Readers' Favorite International book awards.

His other works include *Street Creds*, which details the time he spent in a gang task force. *CurbChek Reload* tells some of the grittiest and most disturbing of the cases he worked. *Hero To Zero* details the incredibly talented cops that he worked with that ended up going down in flames. Some ended up in prison and one on the FBI's ten most wanted list. If you are looking for gritty, true crime stories, be sure to check out all of Zach Fortier's novels.

Zach currently lives in Colorado where he is working on his next book, *I Am Raymond Washington*, which tells the life of the undisputed founder of the Crips gang from Los Angeles during the 1970s.